Praise for *Raising Them*

"An eye-opening and thought-provoking diary of a brave child-reari
adventure, an optimistic and hopeful alternative to the rigid bin:
gender stereotypes that govern child-rearing today."

—Gina Rippon, author of *The Gendered Br*

"A thoughtful, searching, tender exploration of why allowing child
gender freedoms greatly matters—for parents just as much as for ki
With a keen eye on privilege, region, and religion, Myers guides y
with intelligent passion through new terrain. Kids of all genders j
received a gift."

—Kathryn Bond Stockton, author *The Queer Child, or Grow*
Sideways in the Twentieth Cent

"*Raising Them* is a must-read for anyone with children in their liv
Myers gracefully delivers a warm and vulnerable account of parent
that will inspire you to imagine the possibilities of raising a child f
from the gendered expectations that harmfully script everyone's li
experiences."

—Georgiann Davis, author of *Contesting Inter*
The Dubious Diagn

"A deeply personal story that shows how gender creative parenting
work in real life . . . What shines through is how simple gender crea
parenting can actually be. Myers shows that, at its core, gender crea
parenting is about affirming and loving your child, exactly as they
—Christia Spears Brown, author of *Parenting beyond Pink &*

RAISING THEM

RAISING THEM

Our Adventure in
Gender Creative Parenting

—

KYL MYERS

TOPPLE
BOOKS

Little
a

Published by TOPPLE Books/Little A, New York

www.apub.com

Amazon, the Amazon logo, TOPPLE Books, and Little A are trademarks of
Amazon.com, Inc., or its affiliates.

ISBN-13: 9781542003674 (hardcover)
ISBN-10: 1542003679 (hardcover)

ISBN-13: 9781542003681 (paperback)
ISBN-10: 1542003687 (paperback)

Cover design by Philip Pascuzzo

Printed in the United States of America

First edition

For Zoomer Coyote. You made my world better;
now I'm trying to do the same for you.

AUTHOR'S NOTE

I have relied on my memory of these events from this time of my life to the best of my abilities.

I've talked with my family to gather facts and timelines. However, I have changed the names and identifying details of many individuals to protect their privacy.

I use the gender-neutral pronouns *they/them/their* in situations where I don't know the person's pronouns.

A NOTE FROM TOPPLE BOOKS

How do we fight gender norms? We reinvent childhood. Kyl Myers's *Raising Them* is a brave and trailblazing memoir that inspires readers to transform the way we teach our children about gender. Kyl shares their personal story of how they navigate the binary world through a nonbinary lens by practicing gender creative parenting. The book is a candid, eye-opening love letter to their adorable child, Zoomer. Kyl is a bold advocate for the celebration of our growing children's identities, wherever they fall on the gender spectrum.

This book is for people who are passionate about queering parenting. What would the world look like if we allowed people to choose their own identities beyond boy or girl? Who would we be if we were encouraged to play with our genders from a young age? Kyl answers these questions from their own experience raising Zoomer.

As a company at the forefront of the gender revolution, TOPPLE is so excited to see Kyl's vision for the next generation.

—Jill Soloway, TOPPLE Books editor-at-large

PROLOGUE

W hat are you having?"
The question would come out of nowhere. I'd be standing in line at the grocery store or pumping gas, and I'd realize a stranger was staring at my growing belly and in desperate need of knowing my fetus's body parts.

It seemed everyone wanted to know. My friends. My coworkers. Strangers at the movie theater. The person waiting in line at the post office. It was the most common question I was asked during my pregnancy.

Oh, I'm having a human baby, actually, and I'm really excited, I wanted to say.

I never said that, though. *We're going to wait and see. I want to be surprised* was my usual response. People would quickly move on or tell me I was "brave" for feeling like I could prepare for a newborn without knowing the gender. I wasn't quite ready to tell everyone that I had no plans to announce my kid's sex or gender, *ever.*

In fact, if you want to get technical, my partner, Brent, and I had found out our child's sex chromosomes in the very early stages of my pregnancy through a genetic test. But we didn't think those results told us anything about our kid's gender. We imagined it would be years before our child would tell us, in their own way, how they viewed their own gender identity. Until then, we would try our hardest to create a world free of gendered expectations of how children should behave and be treated.

~

Writing this book a few years later, fully entrenched in raising an amazing preschooler named Zoomer, I can say with confidence that I'm *not* an expert in a lot of things related to parenting. I'm not a child nutrition specialist. (We rely on mac and cheese more than I'd like to admit.) I'm not a potty-learning savant. I'm not a sleep whisperer. I'm not a parenting expert. (Who is?) But I do feel like I have one aspect of parenting dialed in: I've kept the promise I made to myself to keep Zoomer's life largely free of gender stereotypes and social and cultural norms based on their reproductive anatomy. I do this for Zoomer, so they can discover their own identity without feeling beholden to the boy-girl binary. But I also practice gender creative parenting because I believe it will make the world a better place. The goal is not to eliminate gender—the goal is to eliminate gender-based discrimination, disparities, and violence. My aim isn't to create a genderless world; it's to contribute to a gender*full* one.

For nearly a decade before the arrival of Zoomer, I was exploring gender with my sociologist hat on. I came to understand the landscape of gender in American culture. Like a geologist analyzing layers of sediment to explain how the land was formed, I studied the layers of social sediment to figure out how gender was formed. I understand *sex* as the biological components of human anatomy and physiology—chromosomes, hormones, reproductive organs, and genitals, for example—and *gender* as relating to social and cultural roles and a person's identity and expression. I believe sex and gender are spectrums; there isn't just one way to be male or female or intersex, and gender doesn't just mean boy or girl or man or woman but includes numerous identities like nonbinary, agender, demi-boy, demi-girl, genderqueer, and so many more. There are as many ways to experience sex and gender as there are humans on the planet. Gender is socially constructed, and how gender is defined and experienced changes across time and geography and will continue to do so.

I've come to understand that gender is one of the strongest predictors of health and economic outcomes, and it's not because of the anatomy someone is born with. It's because of the social pressures, expectations, stereotypes, and restrictions people and systems put on those bodies. From the day a child is born, they are treated differently on the basis of a gender assignment—even though children with vulvas are remarkably similar to children with penises, a cultural norm of biological essentialism leads to children being given different names, different clothes to wear, and different toys to play with; being described with different adjectives; being given different opportunities; and being pushed toward different destinies. Too often, assignments and assumptions are wrong, and individuals have to fight to be recognized for who they really are.

I see the inequities in adulthood—women torn to sexually objectified bits during political campaigns; men told they aren't as capable as women of being great parents; women not getting paid as much as men; men not seeking health care because of the severe pressures of masculinity expecting them to shake off pain, be it emotional or physical; women serving in the military having a higher risk of sexual assault than being injured in combat; men dying in car accidents because they are less likely to wear a seat belt; disordered eating among women; alcohol-induced violence among men; women doing more housework; men being refused time off work when they become a parent . . . I could go on for days. Sexism is also entrenched with racism, classism, ableism, transphobia, homophobia, and nationalism and cannot be seen as a problem that is solvable without addressing intersectionality, or the numerous aspects of a person's identity and how those identities are situated in systems of power.[1]

Yes, there have been monumental strides made toward dismantling the patriarchy and addressing sexism in cultures all across the world. Some societies are making progress toward gender equality faster than others. It is imperative to stay relentlessly focused on things like closing the gender pay gap;[2] electing women and nonbinary people to local and federal offices; eliminating sex and gender discrimination in employment, housing, health care, and other private and public services; eradicating rape culture and toxic masculinity; raising awareness about sex and gender diversity; and protecting trans and queer youth. People's lives depend on it.

While the #MeToo and #EqualPay movements are gaining momentum and dramatic changes are happening in workplaces, there are still baby onesies being sold that say "Lock Up Your Daughters," and girls are earning less allowance than boys.[3] I so clearly see the bread crumb trail from adulthood gender inequalities tracing back to their roots in childhood. I believe societies could have deeper, more long-lasting impacts toward equity and inclusion if they focused just as much on dismantling the gender binary in the elementary classroom as in the corporate boardroom.

Childhood gender socialization is not to blame for gender-based oppression broadly. However, I became so aware of how hyper-gendered, binary, and restrictive childhood socialization is that when I became pregnant, I thought, *No, thank you.* I wasn't about to give in to the binary, the patriarchy, and the status quo and reinforce a tool that maintains systemic gender inequities. I decided to venture off on a path less traveled, looking for a better way.

The good news is that the gender landscape is evolving, and each new generation seems to advance our speed toward equality. It seems the younger someone is, the more they distance themselves from gender norms. The majority of teenagers in the US believe gender is a spectrum, not a binary. One in three teenagers personally knows someone who uses they/them pronouns.[4] And research finds that using gender-neutral pronouns more broadly reduces gender bias.[5] There is exponentially more representation of trans, nonbinary, intersex, and queer folks in the media. The gender revolution is happening, and I am thrilled.

Kids fare better in environments where they are accepted for who they are. The negative outcomes that are often experienced by queer and trans youth are mitigated by loving, accepting, and supportive families and friends.[6] Parents take precautions to keep their children healthy and safe by enrolling them in swim lessons and making them wear life jackets. People teach children to stay away from fire and to stop, drop, and roll. And parents cut food into tiny pieces so their child doesn't choke. Holding space for the possibility a child might be trans or nonbinary or queer is also preventative care.

The generation that my child, Zoomer, is a part of, Generation Alpha, is expected to have a more fluid perspective of gender than any generation before them. It's totally likely that Zoomer might not be cisgender (a person whose gender identity corresponds with their assigned sex at birth), so I want my parenting to reflect that I think that's a possibility and that possibility is A-OK. The possibility of Zoomer being transgender or nonbinary is certainly a part of why I treat them as a child, rather than a boy or girl. I believe Zoomer's gender identity is up to Zoomer to decide, not me.

I have transgender friends whose parents didn't get their gender assignment right. I have an intersex friend whose parents didn't know their daughter had undescended testes and XY sex chromosomes. I know cisgender people who often feel constrained by gendered expectations, norms, and stereotypes. I want to make as few assumptions about my child's gender and sexuality as possible and provide them with the space, safety, and support to explore the sex and gender spectrums, try on different identities, and self-determine what "fits."

Brent and I decided that we would use the singular gender-neutral pronouns *they*, *them*, and *their* to refer to our child instead of the gendered he/him/his or she/her/hers pronouns until they told us what pronouns they want us to use for them. We would not disclose information about our child's genitals to anyone who was not a caretaker or health care provider. We would not subscribe to the constraints of a boy-girl gender binary. We would parent our child in a gender creative, gender-open, gender-autonomous, gender-expansive way.

I want more than half the world for my child. I want all the clothing and toy aisles, not just one section. I want all the colors and activities and books for my child. I want all the adjectives for my child. I want Zoomer to have all the positive experiences and all the opportunities. I want to raise a well-rounded, healthy, happy, compassionate, adventurous, creative, emotionally intelligent, confident, kind, clever, assertive child—and I don't need a gender binary to do that.

∼

I didn't have an in-depth guide for gender creative parenting. I've had to make it up as I go. I have hit a few roadblocks and had to forge uncomfortable detours here and there, but I never encountered any dead ends. I also envisioned the path being lonely, but it has been anything but. My family and friends have rallied around us—Brent, little Zoom, and me. We found community online and in Salt Lake City who have made gender creative parenting not only doable but also immensely enjoyable. That's not to say it's been a total cakewalk. We've had struggles; we've had disappointments; we've had waves of thousands of online trolls. But I've lived to tell the tale, and I'd do it all again.

There's a lot of pressure on parents these days, and my intention isn't to add another dollop of "You should be doing this, not that" to anyone's plate. I am not a perfect parent; I'm just like everyone else, doing the best I can with what I've got. When it comes to parenting tips, it's like drinking from a fire hose, or sixty-three fire hoses, because there is so much conflicting information out there it can be difficult to feel like I'm getting it right. Everyone has different demands on their time; different resources; different privileges and struggles; different relationship structures, backgrounds, and values; and different kids. I also acknowledge that I am in a privileged situation to have the resources and social support that make being a public advocate for gender creative parenting possible.

I'm writing this book in hopes of helping parents who come after me. This book is for people who are tired of the gender binary and all its restrictions and expectations. This book is for people who want to create a more inclusive world for future generations. This book is for people who believe childhood gender socialization needs a radical overhaul and for people who want to contribute to individuality being celebrated more than conformity. This is the book I wish I'd had a few years ago. If something in my story resonates with you, great. If it doesn't, that's OK too.

Hopefully, my story gives permission to adults to interrogate their own identities and try to tease out what about themselves feels authentic and what feels prescribed. After thirty-three years of living life as an assigned girl and woman, I'm giving myself permission to explore my own gender and try on different pronouns, terms, and behaviors. I'm acknowledging that she/her and they/them pronouns fit me best right now, and while I feel very comfortable with my body, I don't know if *cisgender* is a completely accurate term to describe myself. I'm being patient and giving myself space to figure that out and don't feel like I need to hurry. *Queer* is how I define my sexuality, and I stay committed to coming out over and over again, as I am married to a man and my sexuality often feels invisible. Several times in my life, I have encountered a person or a story that has pulled a layer of wool off my eyes and propelled me to level up and think more critically about my surroundings and how I respond to them. I hope my story can be that for someone else.

Every day I witness the results of my conscious actions to prioritize inclusivity and freedom for Zoomer over stereotypes, and I would do it all again in a heartbeat. I'm only a few years into this adventure, but there's no way I'm turning back. I can tell I'm headed in the right direction, and I look forward to seeing you on the trail.

Love,

Kyl

ONE

Meet Zoomer

On a Wednesday afternoon, when Zoomer was two and a half years old, I arrived at their day care to pick them up.

Zoomer's teacher perked up and said, "I have to tell you a story about Zoomer!" I put my backpack down, leaned against the counter, and looked at Abby. This was going to be good. "Some of the four-year-olds were in our class today, and while they were all sitting around tables coloring, one of the older kids asked Zoomer, 'Are you a boy?' and Zoomer looked up at the kid, said, 'No,' and then went back to coloring. The older child paused, then asked, 'Are you a girl?' Zoomer looked back up at the kid and responded, 'No,' and went back to coloring. The curious kid asked Zoomer a final question: 'Then what are you?' Zoomer put their crayon down, looked at the kid, and said, 'I'm a person.'"

Abby smiled. "I thought that was adorable, and I had to tell you." We both looked over at Zoomer, who was sitting across the classroom on the floor, flipping through a book about Komodo dragons. My hand instinctively went up to my heart, and I nodded, feeling a little emotional. "They are an amazing little person, aren't they?"

I believe children's identities are largely influenced by what adults in their lives tell them they are. I have never told Zoomer that they are a girl or a boy. I've only told them that they are a baby, a human, a toddler, a kid, Zoomer, a person. The first time I told them, "You're so special!" they replied, "I not Sospeshul! I Zoomie!" It doesn't surprise me that Zoomer told the child that they are a person, and not a boy or a girl, because that's the language they hear at home. The concrete of a gender binary hasn't dried around Zoomer because it hasn't ever been poured.

Zoomer's favorite color changes often. For a long time, their favorite color was pink; then they went through an orange phase. Their bedroom, wardrobe, and belongings look like a rainbow imploded. They chose the shark water bottle, the *PAW Patrol* toothpaste, and the *Tangled* toothbrush; they wanted the *Cars* Pull-Ups one time and the Minnie Mouse Pull-Ups the next. They picked the pink, purple, and aqua bedsheets; the fire truck socks; the outer space sleeping bag; and the violet climbing shoes. We give them options whenever we can, and they thoughtfully consider the choices and then pick whichever one they like the most. Their decisions don't fall into any stereotypical category or color palette. They aren't under the impression they are supposed to be instinctively drawn to some colors and socially allergic to others.

Zoomer loves dinosaurs, crocodiles, and polar bears and asks me about birds all the time. Which has made me realize I should learn more about birds. Zoomer loves going to the natural history museum and the aquarium. They like watching documentaries about marine life and say to me, "Let's watch an ocean show on the TB, Mommy. You want popcorn?"

Zoomer has a stuffed dog named Dante that goes everywhere with them and a baby doll that they named DeeDee. Zoomer loves Play-Doh and molds neon-colored animals and pretend food. They say, "I'm not going to eat it." And then I see that their teeth are bright blue, and they have, in fact, tried to eat it.

Zoomer is impressively patient with little LEGO builds and helps us find the blocks we need by looking at the instructions pamphlet. They suck the toothpaste off their toothbrush like it's a treat. Zoomer loves having their toenails painted. They rush to the living room window whenever they hear a siren to see which emergency response vehicle is going to drive by. Zoomer has a sugar tooth and tries to negotiate with us daily about cookies.

They love running and dancing and doing gymnastics and swimming. Zoomer adores "sandy areas" and would live part-time in a sandbox if they could. They enthusiastically yell, *"Higher!"* whenever we are pushing them on a swing. Zoomer makes up their own words, blending their mom's and dad's vocabularies. I say *sidewalk*, Brent says *path*, and Zoomer says *sidepath*.

One of Zoomer's favorite things to do is ride their balance bike. Zoomer has a bright-green Strider bike and an orange, black, yellow, and blue helmet with matching riding gloves. When we get home from school, and every single weekend, they ask if they can go on a bike ride. Zoomer cruises alongside us as we walk to buy a bag of coffee beans and asks us to pick flowers so they can decorate their bike. They are impressively good at riding their bike over dirt rollers and berms at the local bike park.

Zoomer sneaks into bed with Brent and me most nights. Sometimes I wake up to them softly rubbing my arm, mimicking how I comfort them; other times I get whacked in the face by an unconscious kid. Zoomer enjoys doing yoga at school, and Brent and I can't help but laugh when they teach us about turtle pose and table pose and rag doll pose and taco pose.

"What's taco pose?" Brent asks.

Zoomer sticks their tongue out and attempts to roll it. "That taco pose," they say.

Zoomer likes picking out their outfit every day, preferring colorful, comfy clothes and shoes they can be active in. Zoomer likes assisting us with chores. They say, "I help you!" and scoot their stool over to the counter and hand me dirty dishes. Zoomer earns pocket money, which they keep in a little sparkly rainbow wallet, and they like to spend their money on tiny monster trucks and fluorescent bath bombs.

Zoomer would eat "mac an cheeses" every day. Zoomer loves going to the city library and picking out new books. They fill up a canvas tote with a dozen books to borrow for a few weeks, and they love returning them, pushing each book through a scanner and onto a conveyor belt, saying, "Goodbye, book! Thank you!" with gratitude. Zoomer has an incredible memory and narrates where we are on our drives and surprises us with facts about the past. Zoomer gives the best snuggles and smooches, and loves when I pretend their foot is a phone. Zoomer concocts imaginative food out of plastic vegetables at their kitchen set: "I make you pineapple smoovie, Mommy. Careful, it's hot. Blow on it." Zoomer gives their classmates big hugs every morning at school, gets bloody noses from rambunctious play, and cuddles their friends when they are sad or ill.

They roar at me and say, "No, thank you!" when they don't want to do what I ask. Zoomer has a great sense of humor and a slapstick-comedy approach to life. Zoomer orders for themself at restaurants. They like mermaids and whale sharks. Zoomer makes up songs and loves dancing to pop music. Zoomer was getting pretty good at hide-and-seek, but once, they ran away from Brent in the mall and ended up on the second floor of a Nordstrom. Brent had to enlist security to seek the hider, and Zoomer hasn't been interested in leaving our side much since. They put on a Rapunzel dress and firefighter hat and shout at the Google Home speaker, "Hey, Google! Play Elsa!" and we help them play "Let It Go."

Zoomer calls my dad, Grandpa Myers, on FaceTime and says, "You want to see my toys?" and proceeds to turn the phone to show Grandpa their train set and dollhouse, bubble bath, soccer uniform, and favorite books as my dad fights back the feelings of seasickness that come with being bounced around on an iPhone for ten minutes and says, "What is this, *The Blair Witch*?"

Zoomer calls pickup trucks "hiccup" trucks, nectarines "submarines," and iguanas "buhgwannas," and I don't think I'll ever correct them.

When I think of Zoomer's personality and interests, nothing about them makes me think, *That's stereotypical* or *That's gender bending*. Gender norms don't get any power in our house. Things are just things, and everything is for everyone. Zoomer is just a kid. An awesome kid.

We've made it three and a half years without gender stereotypes rearing their ugly head in our day-to-day lives, the way I think they would have if we had assigned a gender to Zoomer. Zoomer doesn't seem to know what the gender binary is. And most people don't know what Zoomer's reproductive anatomy is, so they can't plop Zoomer in a binary box. Recently, Zoomer's new teacher, Kimi, told me, "The kids were going around the table today, saying if they were a boy or a girl. When it got to Z, they said, 'I'm Zoomer!' And no one tried to convince Zoomer otherwise."

A friend of mine told me when she first found out how we were going to parent, she thought, *That's going to be endless work for Kyl.* "But now I actually think that you are so lucky and had some great foresight," she told me. "I spend so much of my time tearing the walls down that people are trying to build around my daughters. People aren't trying to build walls around Zoomer because they don't know which walls to build," she confided.

Zoomer knows the words to describe their anatomy, and we encourage them to get to know their body, but Zoomer is not under the impression that their anatomy has anything to do with the types of toys they should play with, clothes they should wear, characters they should pretend to be, friends they should have, or any other aspect of their life. Zoomer is just a little kid who has been enjoying a childhood free of stereotypes. I intend to keep it that way for as long as possible and answer their gender-related questions consciously, age appropriately, and inclusively as they come up.

I notice when someone posts something on social media that relates to children and gender. One parent posted a photo of her Christmas tree with a train set in front of it and said, "After having three girls, I am so glad to finally have a boy so I could buy a Christmas train set." Another parent, after finding out she was pregnant, posted, "Love my boys, but I'm so happy to finally have a girl so I can have a shopping partner." My head tilts to the side a bit when I see these types of posts and a perplexed look comes across my face. Girls can play with trains, and boys can like shopping.

There is liberation in gender creative parenting, for parents and for children. Zoomer gets to like what they like. I never could have predicted that I would have an indie-pop-loving, Play-Doh-eating, fashionable little BMXer, but I do, and I'm excited for the unlimited number of surprises about Zoomer's interests, hobbies, and personality that await, because they are better than anything I could have hoped for.

TWO

An Upbringing Shapes an Upbringing

I was raised Mormon, and in my early childhood, my parents gave me the freedom to express myself the way I wanted. My mom would sew church dresses with matching hair clips that my younger sister Mykenzie and I would wear, but we would immediately change into T-shirts, shorts, and Keds when we got home, and we would play until we were covered in dirt and exhausted. I got to pick out my own clothes and often wore my brother's hand-me-downs, which included neon-colored shirts and parachute "MC Hammer pants."

We spent more time outside than in, and even though my mom rarely left the house without makeup on, she didn't have feminine ideals that I was expected or forced to fit into. It was the early 1990s, and I got to exist between the space of the very gender-neutral 1970s and the hyper-gendered 2000s.

The community of Mormonism was my favorite part about growing up in "the Church" in small-town Oregon. *You're moving?* Twenty-seven people will show up to pack your house up, move you, unpack you, and also leave you a casserole to get you through your first night in your new place.

You're having a baby? All your other kids will be picked up and fed and tuckered out while you give birth and get settled in with your newborn, and then the ward will bring you breakfast, lunch, and dinner for a few weeks.

It's a holiday? We've got a party for that. There were Fourth of July parades, where we'd decorate our bikes and ride around the church block. There was trunk-or-treating around the church parking lot on Halloween. There were ward Christmas parties in the church gym with a potluck feast and a Santa who looked remarkably like Jacqueline's dad—*Hey, where is Jacqueline's dad?*

The Mormon Church was our life. You become friends with the members of your ward, so you automatically have friends at school and people to hang out with on the weekends and free babysitters. The mail carrier is in your ward; the dentist is in your ward. Yet the closeness created a veil of a false sense of safety.

One specific memory of my Mormon childhood stands out. I was in third grade. I had instructions from my mom to walk home with my friend Eric to his house after school. I showed up at Eric's house, and our moms were doing crafty Mormon things—probably making a wreath. I decided to go downstairs to Eric's basement and play Nintendo.

That day I was wearing a short-sleeved white T-shirt and a navy-blue skort with suspenders. I liked how my strong, tanned legs looked in that outfit. It was 1994, and I had just recently asked for a bowl cut *and* a perm, and luckily (or not so luckily), my parents pretty much always let me do what I wanted with my hair.

I was sitting alone cross-legged, playing Mario Bros. as the afternoon sun made its way through the blinds. I turned around and saw Eric's thirteen-year-old brother, Jacob, holding a bowl. I asked him what he had (always scavenging for food I was), and he said, "Nuts."

I paused the game and stood up. "I want some nuts," I asserted and walked toward him with a confident but foal-like gait.

With a crooked smirk across his lips and in a deeper, slower tone of voice, he said, "You want some nuts?" The double entendre went over my head. I confirmed that, yes, I wanted nuts, and I followed him into his room, where he shut the door behind me.

His room was clean, and his queen-size bed was neatly made. He sat down on the side of the bed, closer to the pillows. I had to boost myself up with a little backward jump, and I plopped on the bed next to him and set my eyes on the bowl of mixed nuts.

I grabbed a cashew and put it in my mouth. I could hear my mom talking in the kitchen directly above me, the floor creaking a bit, and chairs making screeching, sliding sounds on the hardwood floor.

Jacob put his hand on the lower part of my back and got a handful of my shirt and pulled it out from its tucked position.

"If you tell anyone about this, I'll kill your dog," he said.

I didn't know what "this" was. I was eight.

"I don't have a dog," I said, laughing.

"Then I'll hurt your mom."

Now I was listening. I still didn't know what "this" was, but I knew it couldn't be good. I was lying down on the bed, with my knobby-kneed legs hanging over the edge, too short to touch the ground. His hand was on my thigh under my skort. His face was closer to mine than anyone besides a family member's had ever been. I didn't know what to do with my arms. His teenage body was twice as big as mine.

"Kylee!" My mom was banging on Jacob's bedroom door. "Kylee, are you in there? Jacob! Open the door!" I knew that I hadn't done anything wrong, but the look on Jacob's face confirmed that he felt like he had been caught doing something he shouldn't, and I was involved . . . so, was I going to get in trouble for whatever "this" was?

Jacob stood me up as Eric got the door open. For a split second, my mom and Eric stood on one side of the open door, Jacob and I on the other.

"What's going on?" My mom looked at Jacob. "Why is Kylee's shirt untucked?"

Jacob stammered, "I . . . I . . . I've never seen a girl with a shirt untucked. I wanted to see."

Even I thought the excuse was weak. My mom grabbed my hand, and we walked up the stairs, collected our belongings, and were out the door and into our Honda Accord.

I was sitting in the back seat, alternating between looking out the window that I was just tall enough to see out of and down to the seat that had a rainbow of melted crayon wax embedded in the gray fabric.

As we drove home, my mom said, "Kylee, I need you to tell me what happened with Jacob." For the first time, probably ever, I didn't know what to say.

She gently pressed again. "Kylee, did Jacob do something to you?"

I thought for a moment and said, "I can't tell you."

My mom asked me why I couldn't tell her, and I said, "Because Jacob said he'll hurt you. First he said he'd hurt my dog, but when I told him I don't have a dog, then he said he'd hurt you."

My mom took a deep breath in and let it out slowly. "Kylee, Jacob is not going to hurt me. I need you to tell me what happened so I can take care of you." So I told her.

A couple of days later, I sat sandwiched between my parents in our living room, the only one in the room whose feet couldn't touch the carpet. Across from us, Jacob sat with his parents. Jacob looked sheepish and cowardly, saying a quiet "I'm sorry" at the prompting of his parents. I'm guessing that everyone considered the issue resolved that night. Everyone but me. I had just learned how powerless I could be with older boys.

~

*W*orthiness is a big deal in the Church of Jesus Christ of Latter-day Saints. At a very young age, we were taught that we needed to be worthy—be obedient and kind and make good decisions that don't cause harm to others, and we needed to be pure in our thoughts and actions. Girls were told that sexual intimacy is reserved for marriage and cautioned against being alone in a room with a boy. We were taught that being sexual with anyone other than our husbands was a sin that was more serious than any sin except murder. Through our worthiness, we would be rewarded, and we could live in the celestial kingdom with Heavenly Father and Jesus Christ and our family for eternity after our time on Earth. Worthiness was on my mind a lot in those days. I had recently been baptized, a rite of passage for eight-year-old Mormon kids. It was an initiation into being accountable for our decisions. Was I accountable for what happened in Jacob's room? Mormon girls are made to feel like sexual gatekeepers, like boys can't help themselves, so it's our job to keep them in check, keep them pure, never tempt them. Even boys who are older? Even in situations that we don't understand?

On the Sunday following the incident with Jacob, I was sitting in church with my family when the sacrament ritual began. A man "blesses" the sacrament (a bunch of torn pieces of bread and plastic thimbles of tap water). Then a gaggle of young men take little trays and pass the sacrament to all the members of the congregation. You aren't supposed to take the sacrament if you did something that week that made you unworthy, that you needed to ponder and repent for. And you sure as hell shouldn't be passing the sacrament if you haven't had a very worthy week.

As I watched Jacob pass the sacrament from pew to pew, I thought, *Wait . . . Jacob shouldn't be passing sacrament this week. He should have taken at least a week off to think about what he did to me. Or am I supposed to be taking a week off because I should have known better? No. That wasn't my fault.* I looked to the small group of church leaders behind the podium, all White men, and caught the eye of Jacob's dad, who was the head of our Mormon ward. In that moment, I realized that optics were more important than worthiness in my church and that I wasn't as important as Jacob. I didn't know the word for it on that Sunday, but I got a taste of the patriarchy with that white bread and water, and I didn't like it.

~

When I was nine, my family moved to Utah, and my parents got divorced shortly after. My older brother, Japheth, and I lived with my dad, and my younger sisters lived with my mom. In my community in Saint George, Utah, girls were expected to grow up to become good Mormon wives and mothers. Getting girls involved in STEM wasn't a thing in my hometown unless by STEM you meant floral arrangement class. It seemed adults were completely oblivious to the fact that girls had the potential to accomplish anything beyond contributing to Utah's fertility rate. Where I grew up, girls were much more likely to be married and pregnant by their twenty-first birthday than attending college.

In the late 1990s and early 2000s, the World Wide Web was just starting to reach southwest Utah. I didn't have a smartphone as a teen-ager, and when I used the dial-up internet on our home computer, it was primarily for downloading music and chatting with my friends on MSN Messenger. My fondest memories of using a computer in school include playing *Oregon Trail* in "computer class," which was taught by an elderly woman who didn't even know how to draft an email. It's no surprise I still have to look at the keyboard when I type. Computers and unlimited access to information weren't a central part of my early educa-tion. My high school seemed more like a place to keep kids occupied during the day than an institution of learning and discovery. I kept my grades and attendance just good enough to graduate, but I was ignorant.

Young Mormon women were encouraged to marry a man who had served a two-year service mission for the Church. With the young men off on missions from ages nineteen to twenty-one, young women needed to find something to do. Not a single one of my girlfriends embarked on the path of the quintessential American high school graduate. None of us applied to universities; none of us got moved into a dorm room by our parents. Some of my friends got entry-level jobs; some started cosmetology school, more as a hobby than a career trajectory; and a few of us, including me, started taking a class or two at the local Dixie State College, which had a very low bar for admittance. *Can you pay? You're accepted.*

My group of friends was gathered one evening, talking about boys, complaining about homework and being broke, and debating whether we should go to a concert in Vegas or "up north" to Salt Lake City to go shopping the next weekend, when Kammie announced she was going to go be a nanny on the East Coast.

"How?" we wanted to know. "What is this nanny gig? It pays?"

Kammie told us about the online site she had found where you could make a profile, search, and connect with families and go be their nanny. Utah-raised nannies were popular on the site. After all, a Mormon babysitter has a ton of experience, is sober, and won't seduce someone's spouse (theoretically).

Within days of learning about this potential ticket out of town, several of us made accounts. My friends viewed nannying as a gap year between high school and hunting for an eternal companion. I was feeling uninspired in my college courses, restless in my small town, and newly aware of how big the world was and how little I knew about it, so I created an account and started scrolling through my options.

I found Marie, a British woman living in Germany. She was a communications professional in her late twenties and looked oh-so-chic. She had a beautiful three-year-old son named Louis, whom she called

Lou-Lou. He had white hair and giant blue eyes and a big smile and was absolutely adorable.

Marie and Lou-Lou lived on a military base in western Germany near the border of the Netherlands. Marie's husband, James, was in the British Army and was currently on duty in the Middle East. Marie was looking for a live-in au pair to come and help her with Louis. All room-and-board expenses would be covered, and the au pair would get an allowance of one hundred euros a week. I messaged her, telling her I was interested. Within a couple of emails, we agreed we were a good fit; within a week, I applied for my first passport and booked a one-way ticket to Germany. My parents took the news well, knowing I was in desperate need of a change of scenery. My dad bought me a big suitcase that I stuffed with half my belongings, and I boarded the plane in Las Vegas two days after Christmas.

During my layover in Copenhagen, I approached the immigration officer and handed over my travel documents. They flipped through my fresh, stampless passport and, in a deep voice, asked me, "Your first time out of the US?"

I nodded and responded with a nervous "Yeah."

They smiled and told me, "I'm honored to be giving your passport its first stamp."

I took my passport back, surprised the Danish agent could speak English so well and feeling self-conscious about my lack of linguistic abilities. "Thanks. Happy to be here."

Marie and Lou-Lou picked me up at the Düsseldorf airport. Lou-Lou was pacing around Marie, wearing Bob the Builder wellies (rain boots) and a blue-and-yellow raincoat over his pajamas. I had arrived at night, and he would be put to bed as soon as we made it home to the base where they lived. Where I was about to live.

I sat in the back of the car with Lou-Lou. He hadn't heard many American accents, and I hadn't heard many English ones. "Hi, Lou-Lou, what types of things do you like to do?" I asked.

Not interested in my question, he asked his own: "Are you going to be my pear?"

I nodded. "I am going to be your au pair. We're going to play and have lots of fun together."

To say Lou-Lou and I hit it off would be an understatement. We were smitten with each other after twelve kilometers. Whenever Lou-Lou struggled to understand my American accent, I would pretend to be a Spice Girl and put on my very best English accent until he got what I was saying. I also had to learn their vocabulary. I'd say a word, and Lou-Lou would furrow his brow, which signaled he had no idea what I was saying—so I'd look to Marie, who would give me the British word. Ketchup = tomato sauce, trunk of car = boot, hood of car = bonnet, living room = lounge, diaper = nappy, etc. This commonwealth vocabulary lesson would come in handy ten years later when I would meet my future husband, Brent, in Australia.

~

My life can be categorized by pre-BBC and post-BBC. Marie would turn BBC News on in the mornings as she got ready for work. She would stand at the sink, putting makeup on in front of the mirror. She could do a perfect cat eye with liquid eyeliner while monologuing about current political issues.

On the first morning I was in Germany, I woke up with a mixture of jet lag and excitement. I walked downstairs and was met by images of a land devastated by a tsunami. The Indian Ocean earthquake had created the Boxing Day tsunamis that killed over two hundred thousand people in fourteen countries. I hadn't ever seen anything like it. At eighteen, I was finally understanding that the world was much bigger than me and my life in Utah, and it was in my best interest to learn about and explore it.

All my friends in Germany were young British soldiers. They took me under their wing and out on the town. I was drinking for the first time, and I credit these second lieutenants for my high tolerance of alcohol now. One night, all my friends piled into a bar in Mönchengladbach, and I was the last in line. I got to the door and showed the person checking IDs my passport.

"American," he said.

"Yes," I answered.

"I will let you into the bar if you can prove you know more about your country than I do." I sat down on a wooden picnic table outside the bar and said, "Then we're going to be here for a while."

He talked to me for twenty minutes; while checking locals' IDs, he told me that he didn't think George Bush was a good president and that Americans should travel more to learn that they aren't as great as they think they are. I nodded. I had voted for Bush's reelection a few months before. It was the first time I had ever voted, just four months after my eighteenth birthday. The Republican Party was practically synonymous with Mormonism where I was from, and my parents never talked about politics. I didn't realize there were other options worth exploring. Eventually, he let me into the bar with my friends, probably out of pity, but my buzz was gone, replaced by a sobering reminder that I was a citizen of a country that wasn't very popular at the moment, and my ignorance was part of the problem.

Meeting Marie changed my life. She was the first woman I met who had a college degree, was fiercely independent and intelligent, was a mom, and unapologetically had a career and made her own money. Marie loved Lou-Lou and invested time and energy into nurturing his interests. She sat in his room in the morning while he made her a plastic breakfast from his kitchen set. They danced to Europop Top-40 music. When I colored Lou-Lou's hair blue and green with markers, she said, "Oh Lou-Lou, you look brill!" She wanted Lou-Lou to do and wear and play with whatever made him happy, even if it didn't align with the military's ideals of masculinity. After nine months in Germany, I decided to return to Utah. I finally felt inspired to care about higher education. I realized that college wasn't a limbo period before marriage; instead, an education was going to be my metamorphosis.

I wanted a degree, independence, and new experiences more than I wanted marriage and children. Those things can coexist, but I knew that if I started a family right away, I probably wouldn't get a degree later. I finally saw some potential in myself that no one else had seen before, or if they had seen it, they hadn't cared to encourage it or had intentionally squashed it.

The push toward social justice, and what would become my life's work, happened in a class at Dixie College back in Utah. It was an English course, and the goal of the class was to improve students' persuasive writing skills. Each week we'd discuss a topic, and then we'd have to write an essay, taking a position on some aspect of the issue. In the class we discussed topics like terrorism and domestic violence, and because we were following a textbook, I looked ahead and saw a chapter on same-sex relationships and marriage equality. I could hardly contain my excitement—I was looking forward to having a discussion with my classmates, the majority of whom were Mormon, about why same-sex relationships should be supported.

I had recently watched as Kammie's older brother, Tyler, came out as gay, and their Mormon mother ostracized him. I noticed Kammie's ideology about queerness and about same-sex marriage became more bigoted, influenced by her mom and her new boyfriend, Paul. I felt heartbroken for Tyler.

I didn't know any out gay people, other than Tyler. But now I was coming to understand why. Being gay and out about it meant risking the loss of relationships with family and friends. It meant losing membership in a culture and community that believe acting on same-sex attraction is a sin. Being gay was shameful and hidden in my small town. My parents hadn't raised me to be homophobic, but I also hadn't been raised to be an explicit ally to LGBTQ issues.

But somehow I was able to form my own opinion as a teenager, and I believed that same-sex relationships were valid and should be supported. I hadn't yet realized that I, myself, was queer. Having grown up in a culture that didn't make room for same-sex relationships, didn't allow them, rarely discussed them, and never discussed them in a positive way, I recognize in hindsight that I had romantic and sexual feelings for girls, but I instinctively bottled them up and ignored them and focused my attention on the boys I was attracted to. A survival mechanism? I grew up in a culture where "pray the gay away" was offered as a solution, where people with same-sex attractions were told that Heavenly Father was testing them, where adolescents were traumatized by their parents forcing them into conversion therapy, where I was taught my purpose in life was to be a wife to a man. Getting out of Utah for a while allowed me to grow as a person, and I had realized that human diversity is a wonderful thing, and being gay or lesbian was a part of that beautiful diversity, and I couldn't be silent on the issue anymore. Finally, my peers were going to have the opportunity to also critically consider their own upbringing and have a chance to form their own opinions.

Then my professor skipped that chapter and went on to the next one, maybe something about cloning. I was disappointed that, in a class called Aims of Argument, I wasn't able to argue about things that were important to me. If anyone needed to learn more about same-sex relationships and come to understand them as valid, it was students at Dixie State College, young people who had attended Utah high schools where discussing homosexuality was restricted under a "no promo homo" law.[8]

I emailed the professor and asked if I could set up a meeting to talk with her. I went to her office and began my prepared speech, meant to convince her that we needed a discussion about same-sex marriage in the class.

"It would be really beneficial to my classmates and me to have some conversations about gay people and the issues they face," I said. "I'm disappointed that we aren't doing that, and by skipping the chapter, I feel like you are essentially telling the class that the issue isn't important or that it doesn't affect them. This is college, and we are supposed to have uncomfortable conversations in college so we can grow as learners and members of society!"

She sat at her desk, letting me vent my frustrations. She took her red-framed glasses off and calmly and kindly asked, "Thanks, Kyl. Are you finished?"

I nodded. "I think so, at least for now."

She told me that the previous semester she hadn't skipped the chapter on same-sex marriage. She said that for the eighty-minute class, the students had spewed cruel, homophobic comments. She had tried to make arguments supporting gay rights but had been drowned out by thirty students shouting at her that gay people are hedonistic sinners who are betraying their God-given roles.

She paused for a moment, looked down, took a breath, put her glasses back on, and told me that her brother was gay, and she loved and supported him very much, and she understood she was a professor who should be challenging students, but she was also a human. Last semester had been pretty traumatic, and she wasn't ready to do it again yet. "What if there is a gay student in my class? I couldn't imagine making them listen to an hour and a half of abuse from a misinformed, hateful, homophobic swarm of students."

I was sorry that happened to her, and I understood why she skipped the chapter this semester. I stood up from the seat, and as I put my backpack on, she told me, "I hope you find what you're looking for."

I took a deep breath and said, "Me too," then left her office.

～

I was working at an insurance agency to pay for my college classes and bills. On a slow day at work, after exploring the majors list on Dixie College's website and feeling underwhelmed by the limited options, I decided to browse majors at other schools. I opened a new browser window on the computer, typed in "UCLA majors," and pressed "Enter." I clicked on the first result, and my eyes bazoinged out of my head. *Wait! What? What are all these majors? You can just go and declare these majors and just learn about these things and get a degree in them?* I took them all in; as I read each major, my brain was like a Richter scale, recording the energy emitted from my body. *Anthropology, Asian religions, biophysics, chemistry, Chicana and Chicano studies, climate science, economics, engineering, geology* . . . My eyes landed on *gender studies* and stayed there. *Gender studies? What's gender studies?* I clicked on the link and was directed to the gender studies department website and got swallowed whole. I was clicking on major requirements and faculty profiles, and I read every single course description. The phone on my desk rang and brought me back to reality.

I was going to major in gender studies. I probably wasn't going to get into UCLA straightaway with my current academic background and abysmal ACT score, but this was it. There was an interdisciplinary field dedicated to the study of gender and how it relates to social identities and institutions. There was an ocean of literature and scholarship that analyzed and challenged systems of power and hierarchies and inequalities, and I wanted in. I could save myself. I did some research and came up with a plan.

Within a matter of days, I had arranged with my aunt Kora to move in with her once the current semester ended. I put in my notice at work, applied for admission to Riverside Community College, and planned to transfer to UCLA later.

Arriving in Riverside, California, I felt like Dorothy in the Emerald City. The Inland Empire is a bit smoggier, but the I-15 was my Yellow Brick Road; there might as well have been a choir singing the "Optimistic Voices" song as I drove in.

I was in Riverside for one incredible year. I saw more people of color on the first day of school than I collectively had in my entire life. I joined Model United Nations and traveled to Xi'an, China, and London, England, and pretended to be a diplomat with people who became my dear friends. I was elected to the student government, where I made more friends, got to represent the student body on a presidential search, and nominated a woman, and I organized an epic "GLOWing back to school" dance. I started volunteering at the Riverside Area Rape Crisis Center. I took my first-ever sociology class, Women in American Society, and, at twenty-one, was befriended by Tara, the first out lesbian I had ever met, who got me involved in the *No on Proposition 8* initiative fighting for the legality of same-sex marriage and is still one of my best friends.

Finally being exposed to how messed up the world is, is a lot to take in when you're a sheltered kid from Utah. My new friends in California were living in poverty; some were struggling young parents; some were undocumented immigrants trying to navigate getting an education.

Most of my days were spent in classrooms, and many of my nights were spent in hospitals assisting survivors of rape. I learned about slavery, colonialism, racism, xenophobia, and the civil rights movement. I learned about sexism, rape, misogyny, and transphobia and was inaugurated into feminism. I learned about heteronormativity, homophobia, the Stonewall riots, and the gay rights movement, all while coming to a new understanding of my own sexuality and realizing I was bisexual.

It was an intense year, to say the least. I started seeing how systems of power were socially constructed and built for White people, men, and wealthy people and how others were oppressed, exploited, and controlled. Once they were exposed to me, I couldn't unsee the inequalities, exclusions, and injustices all around me and also how I had benefited from them. But I also realized that I could fight to dismantle the injustices and work to build something new.

I thought I'd be in a sea of progressives in California, that I'd be in an echo chamber of inclusivity in my new college classrooms, but that wasn't always the case. Same-sex marriage was a hot topic and a very controversial one at Riverside Community College, but at least in all my classes, we talked about it.

A young man stormed out of my Women in American Society class during a lecture about women in politics, yelling that he didn't need to be subjected to liberal lesbian ideology. In my African American History classroom, where I was the only White student, I remained quiet as some Black Christian students argued that same-sex marriage was not how God intended relationships to be, and they were looking forward to voting yes on Proposition 8, to prohibit same-sex marriage in California.

Our professor was the first Black woman to earn a history PhD from her university. She listened to the students' opinions and then stood at the front of the class and gently mentioned that the arguments she was hearing Black students make against same-sex marriage sure sounded a lot like the arguments she'd heard White people making against interracial marriage not too long ago. She told the class, "Don't forget the histories of this country as you walk into the voting booths to create the future."

Three professors at Riverside College paid special attention to me. One was Dr. Langston, my Model UN adviser. After we got back from a conference in London, he asked me, "Have you thought about pursuing a PhD?"

I laughed. I was a country bumpkin from Utah. I didn't even know what *PhD* stood for. But I had been transformed by these three professors: a political scientist, a sociologist, and a historian. I wondered if I, too, might be able to change young people's lives and contribute to their transformation into more socially aware humans.

"I think I'm going to come home," I said on the phone to my dad.

"Oh yeah? What's going on?" he asked.

"I think I'm going to be in school for a long time, and I should probably move to Salt Lake," I said. I wanted to finish my gender studies degree at the University of Utah, with resident tuition, and then apply to graduate school.

My dad rarely opposed or lobbied on behalf of anything I wanted to do. His response was usually something along the lines of "Whatever you think is best for you, Kylee Wylee."

I moved back in with my dad and his wife, April, and quickly finished my associate's degree at Dixie College five years after I started it. For the third time in three years, I loaded up all my belongings into my little Pontiac Vibe and moved to Salt Lake City and started the gender studies program at the University of Utah.

THREE

The Pivot

I was sitting in a feminist theory class at the University of Utah when the professor asked the class to read news articles about Storm, a child being raised without an assigned gender in Canada, and about Sasha, a child being raised without an assigned gender in the UK. I also read Lois Gould's 1978 essay "X: A Fabulous Child's Story."

I read the news articles and the essay, feeling intrigued at first and then inspired. I thought, *This makes sense. What a gift to give a child, the agency to explore gender and live outside the confines of binary stereotypes.*

At the end of the articles about Sasha and Storm, I noticed the comment section. Anonymous commenters from all over the world were saying horrible things about these families. Comments cited religion and the God-given, "scientific" fact that there are only two genders, male and female, and anyone who tries to say otherwise doesn't deserve to parent or, worse, doesn't deserve to live. The transphobia and homophobia and misogyny were palpable. My education had given me historical and scientific evidence that countered the beliefs of this hateful swarm of inaccurate commenters. Peeking into this online vitriol opened my eyes to how far society still has to go to recognize and celebrate the complexities of sex and gender and how important it is to dismantle the patriarchy.

E ven in my gender studies classroom discussions, the concepts of parenting without publicly disclosing a child's sex and not assigning a gender were often touted as utopian ideas, impossible to actually pull off in the real world. I disagreed. Sasha's parents were doing it; Storm's parents were doing it. I imagined there were dozens if not hundreds of other families doing it. With commitment and a metric ton of patience, gender creative parenting seemed completely possible.

I believed the world needed a gender creative parenting movement.

At twenty-four, I wasn't interested in becoming a parent yet. I was determined to finish my degree and become a self-sufficient badass. But there was something about gender creative parenting that appealed to me. I tucked the idea away in my brain, to be retrieved if I ever decided I was ready to become a parent. I also thought, *If I ever become a public advocate for gender creative parenting, I will never read the comments.*

After finishing my gender studies degree, I started a doctoral program in sociology at the University of Utah. For six years, my job in grad school was to read scientific research about social inequities. Over and over again, I saw that the most important predictor of a person's social, health, and economic outcomes was their gender.

I was stunned to learn that men are twice as likely to die from accidents and unintentional injuries as women.[9] Men are also more than three and a half times more likely to die by suicide than women in the US.[10] How men are socialized throughout their lives puts them at a higher risk of accidental, unintentional, and premature death.[11]

These statistics reminded me that boys are still too often raised being told, "Toughen up, don't be afraid, boys shouldn't cry, man up, boys will be boys, don't ask for help." Boys are often molded from a young age to believe that injuries are proof of masculinity, and the more risks you take and precautions you don't, the tougher you are. Accidents happen, but I wondered how many lives could be saved by adjusting what it means to be a boy. If boys were taught from a young age that it's important to know your limits and say "No, I'm good" if something doesn't feel right.

My studies allowed me to see the childhood connections whenever I witnessed gender discrimination in adulthood. I saw where societies could have pivoted and could have done more to help children grasp the concepts of equity, diversity, inclusion, acceptance, kindness, respect, cooperation, and fairness. Instead, I saw how children were separated, pitted against each other, told that gender is either *this* or *that*, and if you're a *this*, then you don't get *that*, and if you're a *that*, then you can't play with *this*. To me, it was no wonder there were so many negative gender-based outcomes in adolescence and adulthood.

Women make up about 28 percent of individuals in science and engineering occupations. In middle school and early high school, there's usually gender parity in science classes, but the pipeline starts leaking later in high school and in college. There are fewer female faculty, and women in STEM fields face more stereotypes and discrimination than their male counterparts. The bread crumbs don't start in college, though; we can find them in kindergarten classrooms and even earlier.

I was frustrated when I learned about stereotype threat, which means that even being aware of a negative stereotype about a group you belong to can negatively affect your ability to perform. When girls are aware of the stereotype that boys are better at math than girls, girls perform more poorly on a math test if they are reminded of the stereotype beforehand. If they aren't reminded of the stereotype, they perform just as well as boys. The older a girl gets, the more she is drenched in reminders of the stereotype that she's not as good at math and science as boys. It doesn't stop at gender. In the last two decades, hundreds of research studies have documented the effects of stereotype threat in regard to race, class, age, and other characteristics and how they overlap.[12]

Stereotypes about "brilliance" emerge early. A team of researchers conducted a study that was published in 2017 in the journal *Science*.[13] The researchers wanted to find out at what age children start buying in to the stereotype that men are more intelligent than women. They recruited kids between the ages of five and seven, and they read each child a story about a "really, really smart person." Then the researchers showed four pictures to the child; two of the pictures were of women, and two of the pictures were of men (adults the children had never seen before). The researchers then asked the child, "Who do you think the really, really smart person was in this story?" Five-year-old boys and girls were equally likely to choose someone of their own gender. A five-year-old girl would point to the picture of a woman and say, "She is the really, really smart person." However, the six- and seven-year-old girls were significantly less likely to choose someone of their own gender than the boys. Six- and seven-year-old boys were more likely to choose one of the men as the "really, really smart person" in the story, and so were the six- and seven-year-old girls, showing that children as young as six endorse the stereotype that men are more intelligent than women.

There's a national discussion around the gender wage gap in the United States.[14] I wish I had been surprised to learn that there's even a gender allowance gap in childhood—with girls being paid less allowance than boys, even when girls often do more chores.[15] Closing the gender pay gap isn't just about teaching girls that the work they do is equally valuable and teaching them how to negotiate; it's also about teaching boys and men to recognize the ways they've benefited from patriarchal, capitalistic, structural norms that give them unearned power and privilege in the corporate setting and at home.

It also bothered me when I thought about the gendered boundaries in childhood. When girls cross over the boundary of what is deemed as "boy territory," they are often celebrated, called tomboys.[16] When boys cross over this same arbitrary gender boundary into what is deemed "girl territory," they can be shamed and even disciplined because of it. Tom*girl* isn't a widely used term. Boys are called sissies and made fun of. Why on earth would a boy ever want to do girl things? Therein lies the problem. Femininity and masculinity are not set up as equal or fluid; they are hierarchical, with boys and men having more power than girls and women.

Childhood socialization is in need of a drastic change if we ever hope to achieve gender equality. This thought went through my head daily in graduate school. I believe children deserve a chance to discover their own identities outside the pressures of a restrictive binary. A chance at having more fulfilling, supportive relationships with one another. A chance at creating and living in a more equitable world.

Still today, some people ask me to prove to them that gender creative parenting will have good outcomes. There is certainly evidence that accepting your child for who they are and loving them unconditionally regardless of how much they do or don't conform to a binary gender assigned at birth have positive outcomes. That said, I would flip that question around. Can anyone prove to me that the traditional way of treating children with vulvas differently than children with penises is having good outcomes? Because I'm not convinced.

FOUR

First Comes Love

In May 2014, I was on vacation in Sydney, Australia. I had just defended my thesis and earned a master's degree in sociology, and I was in desperate need of some fun. I was a semiprofessional online dater at that point in my life. So a few days into my trip, I decided to log on to Tinder and see if I could meet some locals.

Compared to Salt Lake City, Sydney's Tinder selection was a gold mine. A couple of days into swiping, I came across Brent's profile and pictures. He had beautiful thick, black hair with silver-fox sides and impeccable style. There was one photo in particular that caught my attention. Brent was sitting on a motorcycle, wearing sunglasses, and looking away from the camera and toward a setting sun. He had really great jeans on that fit him perfectly. I swiped right on him. I got the "It's a match!" message, meaning Brent had already swiped right on me.

I delight in making the first move, so I pondered my opening line. I had it. I sent him a message: "I like your jeans, and your genes." Within a couple of hours, he got my message and responded. Who wouldn't after that opener? We arranged to meet at a bar at the Sydney Opera House a few days later.

After catching my first glimpse of him in person, I smiled to myself as I approached the patio table where he was sitting, and we slid into a comfortable conversation. We enjoyed a beer at the Opera House and then went on a walk through the Rocks district to another pub with a rooftop bar. As we drank another beer, I spotted a structure on the far side of the bay.

"What's that building over there?" I asked. "It looks very . . . phallic."

"I'm not totally sure. Probably a lighthouse," Brent replied. I gulped the rest of my pint and suggested that we go find out.

We walked to Circular Quay, the main ferry terminal, and bought a six-pack of beer from a kiosk and two ferry tickets to Rose Bay. It was late afternoon on a Wednesday, and there weren't many other passengers on the ferry. Brent and I sat on a seat together in the open air, popped the caps off our beer bottles, and clinked them together, making a toast to how well our first date was going. Brent leaned in and kissed me for the first time.

The sun was starting to set as we arrived at the wharf. We didn't know where we were going, but we figured "up" was the right direction. We jumped on a bus that took us up the hill a couple of kilometers. When we got off the bus, I walked to the sidewalk and realized Brent wasn't behind me. I turned around and watched him helping an elderly woman onto the bus. *Oh shit.* I thought to myself, *He helps old ladies onto buses. I'm in trouble.* I knew he was doing it because he wanted to do it, not because I was watching, because he didn't think I was watching. And *that* is a sign of a good human.

My body was responding to everything about him—his height, his thick head of hair, the symmetry of his face, his espresso-colored eyes and long, dark eyelashes, his kindness, his sense of humor, his spontaneity, his conversation skills, his curiosity.

We walked through dark alleys and lamplit streets in search of the lighthouse. Having drunk quite a bit of beer, we both stopped to pee, Brent behind a tree and me in between two parked cars. After a few close calls with giant spiders in suburban webs, I saw it: Macquarie Lighthouse.

It was 6:00 p.m. in Sydney, and the autumn sun had set. The lighthouse was illuminated by spotlights on the grounds. There was a perfectly manicured, emerald-green lawn surrounding the lighthouse that dropped off near the cliffside overlooking the Pacific Ocean. Brent and I lay down on the grass, slightly buzzed on beer but pretty drunk on infatuation. We had our first proper make-out session and soaked in the fun of our chemistry without paying mind to the fact that we lived on different continents in different hemispheres.

While lying on the grass, watching the reflection of the moon ripple on the sea, Brent said, "I'm coming to the States in July. I'll be there until October." A huge smile came across my face, and I told him that was exciting, and I'd of course love to meet up with him somewhere on his trip. Little did we know we'd be living together by August and married in November.

We had only a week together in Sydney, and we made the most of it. We saw each other every chance we could. We had picnics on docks during his lunch hour, laugh fests in bed, street food in Chinatown, and long walks and copious amounts of coffee in Bondi. I cried into the little drink napkin on the plane home. I had a feeling I'd just met the person I wanted to create a life with, and that stirred up some emotions I didn't know I had.

Brent and I spoke every day for two months. The sixteen-hour time difference gave us a very specific communication schedule. Brent sent a "good morning" message before he went to sleep. I woke up to start a day he had just finished in Australia. We would FaceTime in the afternoon, Utah time, when Brent was just waking up, then again when I was getting ready for bed and Brent was taking his lunch hour. We used an app called Couple on our phones. We could message each other and send pictures and drawings. I also sent Brent a postcard every single day; he kept them, and the stack now sits in a drawer in our bedroom. We were making the most out of a long-distance situation and trying to get to know each other as best we could. During those two months, I got to know Brent better than I had gotten to know most people I dated. There was something about a long-distance relationship that forced me to dive in. We weren't able to sit in silence and watch a movie next to each other. All we had was communication, so we got good at it.

Brent spent the first part of his US trip in New York with one of his best friends. About a week later, he flew to Salt Lake City and planned to spend six weeks or so with me while I had the summer off from graduate school and teaching. I met him at the airport and couldn't believe I was seeing him in person after our one-week whirlwind romance and two months of FaceTime. He had a backpack and two duffel bags, and he was ready to see where this fling with an American would go.

I had spent the last week getting rid of as much of my stuff as I could. I donated clothes to a women's shelter and made room for his belongings in the tiny closet. I deep cleaned every square inch of my apartment. I scrubbed the kitchen ceiling with a Magic Eraser. I'd never cleaned a ceiling for anyone. I obviously had some intense feelings for Brent. Ceiling feelings.

I brought him back to my one-bedroom apartment, which was now *our* one-bedroom apartment, and we embarked on having a summer together. We visited national parks and traveled to Portland and the Oregon coast. He met my family and won them over. He met my friends and won them over too. We said "I love you" in my friend's backyard during a summer barbecue. We hosted a costume party at our apartment. I was Frida Kahlo, and Brent was "Thunder from Down Under." Our guests received tickets that they could cash in at some point during the night—a lap dance from Thunder or a portrait drawn by Frida. We were a great duo.

It quickly became clear that we wanted to be together, not just for this summer but for every summer indefinitely. I was starting my third year of my PhD program in August and was not in a position to move to Australia. Brent realized if he wanted to be with this Utahn, he would need to be in Utah.

On Halloween, five months into our relationship, while eating schnitzel and drinking a stein of beer at Bohemian Brewery, I asked Brent, "Should we get married?"

Brent smiled and put his beer down and asked me, "Do you want to get married?"

"I believe I do, yes. Do you want to marry me?" I asked.

"I do want to marry you." Brent grabbed my hand and asked me, "Did you just propose to me?"

We both laughed. It was the least romantic, most pragmatic proposal that I could imagine for myself. But we were in love, and we were a great partnership. Getting married made sense. My thinking was that if we couldn't commit to being together and getting married, Brent would return to Sydney, and distance would eventually tear us apart.

There's a line in the movie *The Proposal* with Sandra Bullock and Ryan Reynolds, where Ryan's character (an American) proposes to Sandra's character (a Canadian in need of a green card). He says, "Marry me. Because I would like to date you." We decided going all in and doing the damn thing was necessary if we wanted to be together.

We called the Honorable Judge Karlin S. Myers, a.k.a. my dad, and we told him we were going to get married. We asked if his backyard would be available the Saturday after Thanksgiving and if he would be willing to marry us. Our families were supportive and expressed their excitement for us, but they were likely thinking, *What the hell are these two doing?*

During our four-week engagement, my friends and family tried to help me plan my perfect wedding. But there was no such thing as a dream wedding for me. I hadn't considered myself the marrying type, and I definitely wasn't the big traditional wedding type. I didn't want fancy flowers. I wanted a few succulents for the tables. We didn't need tablecloths, just some butcher paper and markers for the guests to draw with. We didn't want a bridal party, and food was simple; we ordered catering from a local Mexican restaurant, and Brent and I bought inexpensive rings for each other on the internet.

The night before our wedding, I reminded my dad that I would not be changing my last name.

"Dad, don't introduce us as Mr. and Mrs. Courtney. I came into this world Kyl Myers, and I intend to leave as Kyl Myers too."

"That doesn't surprise me one bit," he said.

I found a navy-blue jumpsuit at a boutique for a hundred dollars. It had thin spaghetti straps and a plunging neckline. It even had pockets. There was something about getting married in pants with pockets that helped me feel more comfortable about inviting the government to get involved in my romantic relationship. It was on my terms. I was just a feminist entering into a partnership and doing the celebration my way—the editor of any bridal magazine would have been mortified seeing how little I cared about the traditional frivolous and expensive details. I got ready at my sister Mykenzie's house. My mom helped curl my short hair while I did my own makeup, and then everyone gathered at Dad and April's house. It was wedding time.

Brent and I got married on Saturday, November 29, 2014, sur-rounded by twenty-five of our family members and closest friends and with Brent's family in attendance via FaceTime on an iPad. Brent and I danced down the grassy aisle to the song "Rather Be" by Clean Bandit, and my dad made some cute, thoughtful, and humorous open-ing remarks. Brent read his vows and gave me the pair of his jeans I had commented on in my opening line to him on Tinder; he told me, "You can have my jeans, and as for the other genes, I'll give those to you whenever you're ready."

I read my vows, which included a silly mathematical probability model, where I factored in different variables that contributed to our compatibility, like Brent being between the ages of twenty-nine and thirty-nine and English-speaking and considering himself a feminist. We had huge smiles on our faces during the entire ceremony; we ate tacos, drank tequila, and danced on my parents' patio until midnight. I knew my dad would appreciate me doing one traditional thing, so I asked him what song he wanted to dance to for our father-daughter dance. He said, "That new Katy Perry song." I laughed and told him, "You obviously haven't listened to the lyrics, but screw it, let's do it." So my dad and I danced our asses off to "Teenage Dream" under the desert sky.

Toward the end of the night, we all put sweaters on and roasted marshmallows on the fire pit. After all the guests went home, Brent and I walked a few blocks to the Seven Wives Inn, where we took a bath in the giant 1980s in-room spa tub, ate leftover *tres leches*, and had no-frills drunk wedding sex before falling asleep. It was official. I was married to someone I'd met six months before, and it felt right.

Brent and I decided to share the responsibilities of running a household and have conscious conversations about our daily tasks. I'd catch myself sometimes, right before shouting out to Brent for help with something. *I can change the damn light bulb,* I'd think to myself. And I'd grab a chair and change the damn bulb.

Brent and I wanted to make sure we didn't fall into stereotypical traps of gendered roles. We had our growing pains, but we were determined to make sure neither of us felt like one was doing more than the other. We alternated who made dinner each night and who did the dishes. We did our own laundry. We both mowed the lawn. Brent mowed the lawn in a Speedo, though, so it was tempting to just delegate that to him, demand it be done twice a week, and sit on the porch sipping iced tea watching all six feet, four inches of him zigzag across the yard. We tried to find the balance between what needed to be done, who hated what more, and what genuinely made us happy. Our household to-do lists are a Venn diagram of what's fair and our interests.

My love language is a beautiful color-coded Excel spreadsheet, and Brent's love language is Best Buy. In the Courtney-Myers house, I handle most things that have to do with budgeting, and Brent handles most things that have to do with electronics. But then we give each other a tutorial, so if anything ever happens to one of us, Brent knows how to log in to the EveryDollar app, and I know how to change the batteries in the keypad lock.

Brent had to adjust to living in the US. I had to teach him how American banks worked and how to write a check. We had to talk about money and combine finances early in our relationship. For Brent to get a bank account in the US, I had to be the primary account holder because he didn't have a social security number or any credit history. He was (and still is) frustrated with the complexities of the US health-care system (and rightfully so; do not get me started on the medical-industrial complex), and I had to teach him how to navigate health insurance in America.

At the beginning of our relationship, we were broke. My graduate student stipend kept me hovering just above the federal poverty level. Brent was an incredibly talented graphic designer, but it took a year for him to find a good job and start working his way up to an art director position and then on to a successful freelance career. Within a few years of being married, we had found some footing economically, and after I finished my PhD, my salary grew like a hard-earned magic beanstalk.

"Does it bother you that I make more money than you?" I asked Brent after my paycheck got larger than his.

"As long as I can always buy the newest Nikes," he joked, "I don't care where the money is coming from." He genuinely didn't feel uncomfortable with me earning more money than him.

After my parents' divorce, and watching them struggle to make ends meet, I promised myself that I would be self-sufficient. I was terrified of relying on someone financially. I felt much more comfortable with the idea of being the *provider* rather than the *provided for*. I had made it very clear to Brent that it was unlikely that I would ever put my own ambitions and ability to earn money on the back burner to support his. My life history had made it difficult for me to feel like any situation was guaranteed.

Brent has never acted like his career is more important than mine. Unfortunately, there have been times when Brent has lodged that complaint to me. I don't believe that my career is more important than Brent's, but shaking off a twenty-year-long habit of resisting dependence is a difficult thing to do.

To even consider having a baby, I had to feel confident that Brent would equally share parenting, that he would be a hands-on, involved dad. I had to trust that I wouldn't be the default parent staying home if our child was sick. I knew what the motherhood penalty was, and I'd be damned if it was going to make a statistic out of me.[17]

It's unfortunate how many assumptions are made in relationships, only to find out when it's too late that an assumption was wrong. Some people get married before asking their partner if they want children and, if so, how many. Some people get pregnant before having a discussion about parenting values, and then tension arises because of different parenting styles. Some people have children before having conversations about equally shared parenting, then one parent, often a mom, feels overwhelmed by the responsibilities of parenting without an equally involved partner.

I had seen this happen to people in my life and witnessed the stress it caused. I was determined to be on the same page with Brent before it could become a stressful situation. If Brent wanted to have six kids, I probably wasn't the person he should be with. And if Brent had been the type of person who expected me to be a stay-at-home parent, I would have ended the relationship. If Brent had shown any sign of an aversion to things like changing diapers or a crying baby, I would have thanked him for our time together and moved on.

Before committing to a serious relationship with each other, Brent and I established that we wanted one child, maybe two, definitely not three, but probably just one. We established that we would both parent equally, and I would not be the primary caretaker simply because I was a woman. We agreed that both our careers mattered, and we would be a dynamic-duo tag team, equally sharing parenting and supporting each other in our goals outside the home.

Brent and I also had discussions about the type of parents we wanted to be. We talked about the fun stuff, like how we wanted to travel the world with our kid, and we talked about the not-as-much-fun stuff, like how spanking is absolutely not OK. It wasn't long before we had the talk about gender creative parenting.

We were in construction-induced stop-and-go traffic on the I-15 from Salt Lake City to Las Vegas. It was early September 2014. We were headed to Vegas to meet up with Brent's sister, Kimberley, who was visiting from Australia and traveling the States for a couple of weeks. We weren't trying to get pregnant yet, but the conversations about parenting were becoming more frequent.

"Did you ever read the news stories about Sasha and Storm? The kids whose families didn't assign a gender to them?" I asked Brent from the passenger seat as he drove down the freeway. A picturesque backdrop of the bright-orange sandstone of the Valley of Fire State Park was behind him.

"Nope," he said as he glanced in my direction. "Tell me more."

"A few years ago, there were two different families in the news. Storm is a kid who was born in Canada, and Sasha is a kid who was born in the UK," I started. "Both of the kids' parents didn't assign a gender when they were babies, they didn't publicly announce what type of genitals their kid had, and they didn't say 'We had a boy' or 'We had a girl'; they just said, 'We had a child.' The families were trying to create an environment for the child to grow up in where they wouldn't experience gender stereotypes or expectations or restrictions from the beginning and were just free to explore their interests and become who they wanted to be."

Brent was listening, nodding. "Go on," he said.

"I read about these kids years ago," I continued. "This way of parenting has stuck with me ever since. Now that I am starting to consider becoming a parent and what type of parent I would want to be, doing what Storm's and Sasha's parents did feels the most in line with my values and perspective about gender."

By that point, Brent was very aware of my perspective on gender. By dating me, in a way, he was signing up for an intensive sociology of gender class. In fact, one of the greatest compliments I've received from Brent was when he told me how grateful he was that he had met me, that I had altered the way he thought about the world, and he was better for it.

As I told him about Sasha and Storm, Brent didn't shoot me down from the sky. He smiled and said, "It makes sense." He paused and took a breath. "Talk me through it a bit more. How would this play out in our life?"

"I think as soon as someone knows if a child has a penis or a vulva, there is an unstoppable machine that gets set in motion. It starts with the words we use to describe a tiny human. Even though we know transgender and nonbinary and intersex people exist, there's an obsession with penis equals boy and vulva equals girl, and once that's established, then the kids get placed on different social conveyor belts and sent through life. The boys get blue and black things and sporty things and are molded to be tough and clever, and the girls get pink and sparkly things and flowery things and are molded to be sweet and pretty, and these children, who are actually incredibly similar, are treated very differently just because of their reproductive organs. Then we end up with this socially constructed, artificial idea that men are from Mars and women are from Venus, when in fact we're all just humans from Earth." I paused.

Brent jumped in. "You're always telling me about all the studies you are reading, about gender being such a huge factor in people's health. It's like our society creates these problems and then acts all confused, like 'How did this happen?'"

"Exactly," I said, smiling. *He gets it.* "I see how gender inequities in adulthood can be connected back to childhood gender socialization. I don't want that path for my kid or any kid."

We talked about how cisgender people need to change their behavior if they want to contribute to a world that is not only more equal for cisgender people, but also more inclusive, accepting, and safe for transgender and nonbinary people.

"So if we decided to parent this way, who would know our baby's anatomy? Just us?" Brent asked.

"I think we would just have to be mindful, and only people who really need to know, like a pediatrician or a babysitter, someone who is changing diapers, should know. I think our families could know later, but it would be great if, for a little while, people could just interact with the kid without knowing what their genitals look like, because if they don't know, they can't put our kid in a box." I didn't have all the answers, but I was confident that they would come.

"How would we talk about the baby?" Brent asked.

"Like what pronouns would we use? I know people who use *they* and *them* as a pronoun, and out of all the different gender-neutral pronouns, I think those would be the easiest for our families and other people to get used to." Our conversation was clarifying to me that this was the direction we needed to go as parents if we became parents.

"You know so much more about the topic than I do." Brent looked at me. I could see his eyes through his black Wayfarer sunglasses. The look on his face reminded me of standing on a high dive, wanting to jump into the pool below but nervous. The jump will happen, but there is a moment before the leap. You aren't completely ready for your feet to leave the board, but you aren't going to turn back either. His lips parted, and he hesitated for a moment before speaking.

"I think it's a good idea, but I would have to lean on you a lot to learn how to talk about it. You teach this. You read about this all day. I'm on board, but I'm not as confident in my ability to explain it as you are." He continued, "It isn't the actual practice of parenting this way that scares me; it's having to deal with people who don't agree with it."

He was willing to do this with me. And I was willing to take on the work of strategizing how to do this with him. We left it at that for the day. I was grateful that we had time on our side. I wasn't pregnant. Maybe the fact the baby was hypothetical and there was no impending due date made things easier to talk about.

FIVE

Then Comes Baby

B rent and I were sharing sweet and savory breakfast dishes at the Copper Onion when the baby conversation got real. We knew we wanted to be parents; now we just had to decide if there was such a thing as the right time to become parents.

"The academic world is wonky, and I do think there are better times than others to have a baby in the first part of an academic career." I was trying to explain the trajectory of a professor to Brent and what I was watching happen in the sociology job market. Brent ate pancakes and listened intently.

"I'll be applying and interviewing for assistant professor jobs for almost a year before I would start the job. I don't really want to be mega pregnant or in the newborn stage if I'm going to be flying all over the country interviewing. I think I would rather either have a baby already and be kind of in the groove of parenting or in the very early stages of a pregnancy, like, first, maybe second trimester. If we don't already have a kid by the time I start a job, I think I would want to wait a few years to have a baby and take family leave because I will be working my ass off in the first three to five years as an assistant professor, and I don't think I would want to take a leave and stop my tenure clock."

Brent gave me a puzzled look. "I don't really want to wait five more years and be close to forty when I have my first kid. I want to be a youngish dad, and I'm not getting any younger. So if what you're saying is we either try now or five years from now, then I vote now."

I had never had this type of conversation in my life before. It felt so bizarre to be sitting in a restaurant, actually discussing having a baby. I took a sip of my coffee and leaned back in my chair. "There's no guarantee I'll get pregnant right away. But if I do, it means this time next year, there will be a kid with us at breakfast."

Brent smiled. "Yeah, that is simultaneously exciting and terrifying. You'll be a great mom, and we both know I'll be a phenomenal dad . . . so, let's do it," he said, with a smirk on his face, and took another bite of pancake.

It was the spring of 2015; we'd been together almost a year and married for five months. We were in love, we had a strong relationship and big dreams, and we wanted to be parents. I made an appointment to get my IUD removed.

My fifteen-year-old sister, D'Covany, was living with us for a semester during high school, and one night as we made dinner, I mentioned I was going to have my IUD removed in a couple of weeks so Brent and I could try to get pregnant. She jokingly asked, "Are you going to make a paper chain?"

I paused and thought for a moment and said, "That's a great idea! Want to help?"

Paper-chain countdowns bring me joy. I remember making construction-paper chains to count down to Christmas Day, tearing off a link every morning when I woke up. As a kid, I'd get so excited, I would make a bargain with myself: *I'll tear off two links today, and then I just won't tear one tomorrow.* As if that would make the big day come faster.

After dinner, D'Covany helped me cut links of paper and suggested, "Instead of there just being a final link, I think on the last day, you have to pull a paper IUD out of a paper uterus." We laughed, and then, because it was obviously a genius idea, we got to work drawing a uterus and fallopian tubes and ovaries, cut a tiny little IUD out of paper, and lightly taped it on the uterus. The masterpiece was hung on the doorframe, with fourteen interconnected paper circles running down the wall.

At twenty-eight, I was a bit more patient than I'd been when I was six and a half, so I didn't skip ahead and tear two at a time. Each morning, I would wake up, get the coffee started, and look at the chain, slowly tearing off a link every day. On the day of my IUD removal appointment, I was filled with a nervous excitement. I hoped everything would be OK. I hoped becoming pregnant wouldn't be a struggle. I hoped I'd have a healthy pregnancy. But most of all, I hoped I'd be a good parent.

My period arrived in June, signaling to me that our efforts in May hadn't produced the results we were hoping for. I had been having sex for the last decade hoping not to make a baby, and now I was rooting for my body to do the opposite. It was the first time that my period wasn't a relief. I realized I didn't have a twenty-eight-day cycle but a thirty-one-day cycle, and I adjusted my fertility tracking app accordingly. We would try again in June.

On July 9, the day before my twenty-ninth birthday, I sat down in a chair in the dining room across from Brent, who was working on his laptop. "I'm going to take a pregnancy test tomorrow morning," I told him.

"OK," he said, closing his laptop and turning to face me.

I paused for a moment before continuing. "I feel like the only thing that I have been thinking about for the last ninety days is my fertility. It's a little overwhelming, so I'm going to take the test tomorrow, and if I'm not pregnant, maybe we can restrategize and just have sex when we feel like it instead of when an app tells us to?"

Brent smiled. "That's fair. Anything you want, babelove."

I stood up, feeling relieved, and said good night. I was tired and went to bed.

The next morning, I woke up another year older. Drinking alcohol is a hobby of mine, and even more so on my birthday, so I wanted to know if there was a blastocyst in my body or not before I got on the drink. I got out of bed, grabbed a pregnancy test out of the closet, and made my way into the bathroom. I opened the wrapper, not needing to read the instructions; I knew the routine after last month. I peed on the fibers on one end of the test. I rested the test on the sink, pulled my underwear up, and washed my hands. I sat on the edge of the bathtub, reading the ingredients on a shampoo bottle and counting in my head for two minutes.

I stood up and grabbed the test. There were two blue perpendicular lines, like a plus sign. I took the eight steps from the bathroom to our bedroom. Brent was sitting up in bed.

"Happy birthday!" he said as I walked in.

My face must have looked weird.

"What?" he said, before noticing what was in my hand. "Are you pregnant?"

I took a deep breath and nodded my confirmation. "I'm pregnant."

~

Brent had planned a scavenger hunt for my birthday. He gave me an envelope with the first clue, and inside of it was a tiny flag. On one side was Japan's flag, and on the other was Mexico's flag. Whether it was in my head or real, within an hour of finding out I was pregnant, I was suddenly nauseous. I stared at the flag for a moment, trying to figure out the riddle. "Oh! I know! Sushi Burrito! But I think I would vomit if I had to eat a sushi burrito right now." I looked at Brent with disappointed eyes.

Brent laughed. "We aren't eating at Sushi Burrito, but it is where your next clue is." Over the next couple of hours, Brent drove me around

Salt Lake City as I solved riddle after riddle and found clue after clue at places that had some type of significance to us. The final note sent us to Red Butte Garden, a botanical garden and arboretum, where Brent laid out a picnic spread of my favorite foods. We sat in the shade near a water feature and ate chips and salsa and lox bagels and drank lime Perrier. We watched lizards run across sandstone paths and into perfectly manicured hedges. I no longer felt nauseous, but my body felt tingly with a subtle flow of adrenaline. *I'm pregnant,* I kept thinking to myself.

In the garden's gift shop, Brent found a cute little quail stuffed animal that, when squeezed, made the sound of a quail's call. I had loved watching Brent become fascinated with North American animals over the last year. He'd take photos of a herd of deer that made their home in a local cemetery. He would stand in our front yard and watch squirrels running up trees and along power lines with a giddy smile on his face. "I've noticed that male quails are really involved in taking care of their young," he said to me while looking at the toy. "I'm going to buy this for the baby."

As Brent walked to the cash register, I sent the first telepathic thought to the bunch of cells implanted in my uterus. *You're a very lucky kid.*

~

I had always been into unusual names and kept a running list in my notes app on my phone to keep track of all the cool names I heard over the years. Some names in my notes were Rousseau, Copeland, Phelix, Forest, Petrichor, Schuyler, and Argon and Neon. (Wouldn't those be great names for twins?) The last entry in my notes, made on August 9, 2014, at 6:34 p.m., was Zoomer.

Brent and I were coming home from a restaurant one night a couple of months before we got engaged, and I asked him if he had any nicknames as a kid. As he unlocked our front door, he said, "My parents called me Zoomer."

I melted into a pile of love gloop and immediately said, "If we ever have a kid, we should call them Zoomer." And it just stuck.

To me, *Zoomer* was special. It was a tribute to Brent and also such a fun and quirky word and not gendered. I put it in my notes, and from then on, whenever we talked about the hypothetical child who was a mere twinkle in our eyes, we called them Zoomer. Eleven months later, Zoomer was conceived.

Zoomer's middle name came from my own nickname. When I told Brent that my dad called me (and still calls me) Kylee Wile E. Coyote, Brent was convinced.

"Well, that's it! They'll be Zoomer Coyote, a mixture of their mom and dad."

I did a little bit of research on coyotes, to make sure they weren't perceived as the worst animals ever. Had my nickname been Seagull, it certainly wouldn't have made an appearance on our child's birth certificate, because seagulls are assholes, a determination I had made as a six-year-old when one stole my chicken nugget while I was eating a Happy Meal outside a McDonald's on a family road trip.

Turns out that coyotes are incredible animals. Coyotes are resilient to modern human behavior, and in fact, coyotes can adapt to human environments and thrive within them. Coyotes are flexible in social organization; they can live with their families or in packs of unrelated coyotes, and they don't have many enemies. Coyotes are beautiful animals, and I grew up hearing their howls in the deserts of southern Utah. I loved the idea of raising a little Zoomer Coyote.

～

The day after the positive pregnancy test, the puking began. *Morning sickness* is a misleading term, because I puked morning, noon, and night. No time of day was off-limits when it came to my nausea.

I reached out to the chair of the sociology department to make some changes to my teaching schedule. I would be having a baby in March, in the middle of the spring semester, so we needed to figure something out. We decided that instead of teaching criminology in the fall and gender and sexuality in the spring, I'd teach both in the fall, early in my pregnancy.

During the entire first month of classes, I would throw up in a garbage can or a toilet somewhere on campus before walking into my classroom. I was in the first trimester and wasn't telling people that I was pregnant yet. Those poor students must have thought that their instructor was terrified of public speaking as she walked in each day, no color in her face, having to stop and hold on to the sides of the podium, taking deep breaths, trying to will the vomit away.

After teaching criminology, I'd prep my online gender and sexuality class, get home around 3:00 p.m. every day, and collapse onto the couch. I'd never felt so exhausted in my life. Every time I threw up, it was like my intelligence was being expelled from my body too. I was a weepy, hungry, tired, nauseous, brainless mess. I have a hard time trusting anyone who says they enjoyed pregnancy. That first trimester was brutal.

The smell of coffee wafted out of the drive-up window of Coffee Stop as the barista slid it open to take our order. "Hey, you two! Good morning! What can I get you?" Jean had a welcoming smile and big blue eyes. She had tattoos on her arms and a beanie covering the top of her long, light-brown hair. Brent ordered his usual latte. From the passenger side, I asked for an iced coffee.

"We're going up to Park City to get out of the heat," Brent told Jean.

I joined in. "What about you? Any plans for after work?"

"I'm going home and going straight to bed! I had a birth last night and have been up for over twenty-four hours." Her pep did a convincing job covering up her exhaustion.

"Sorry . . . you had a birth last night?" Brent asked, astonished and concerned.

Jean threw her head back as she laughed. "Not my birth! My client's birth. I'm a doula. Sorry, that was not clear at all. No, I did not have a baby last night." We all chuckled.

She passed our coffees through the drive-up window, and Brent grabbed them and put them in the cup holders.

As we rolled the windows up and waited at the traffic light, I said, "She's a doula."

Brent nodded while enjoying his scorching latte on a ninety-degree day. "Yeah, are you thinking you want her to be our doula?"

I wanted to have a home birth, and we were looking for a midwife and a doula. I took a sip of the cold, black coffee and reluctantly admitted to myself that, unfortunately, coffee did not seem to be mixing well with my pregnant body. "I am thinking that. I'll ask her if she's interested the next time I see her."

"Great!" Brent said. "I like her. I feel like she would probably be a great fit for us." Brent looked over at me and then did a quick double take. He grabbed my hand with a concerned frown. "Kyl Myers, don't take this the wrong way, because you know I think you're gorgeous, but you are not looking OK right now."

"I can't drink this coffee." I frowned, looking at the full cup. "Growing a fetus is hard work, and now I can't even do it caffeinated."

I retired the coffee to the cup holder, took a deep breath, and rolled the window down for fresh air, wishing the incessant feeling of seasickness would fly out of the car.

A few days later, I walked to Coffee Stop with two missions in mind. First, I was going to figure out what my new beverage of choice would be during my nauseous first trimester. Second, I was going to ask Jean to be my doula. I strolled up to the walk-up window and was met by Jean as she slid the glass open with a smiley "Hey, friend!"

"Hi, Jean," I responded. "My name is Kyl, by the way. I don't know if I've ever introduced myself to you."

"Nice to officially meet you, Kyl. What can I get you to drink?"

"Well, I'm pregnant, and coffee is making me queasy and is very unappealing at the moment, which makes me a bit sad. So I'd like an iced drink that's not coffee. Do you have any recommendations?"

Jean's eyes lit up. "You're pregnant! That's exciting! When are you due?"

"March nineteenth. I'm in the early days of the first trimester . . . and throwing up a lot and feeling like shit."

Jean nodded. "Feeling like shit in the first trimester sucks, but your body is making another body, and that's pretty incredible, so be easy on yourself."

"That's what I try to tell myself as I'm heaving over a toilet every day: 'You're making a spine, Kyl. This is worth it!'"

We both laughed in a solidarity of sorts.

Jean suggested a drink. "You should try the ginger twist iced tea. It's lemonade and tea with some ginger flavor, which is good for helping with nausea."

"Sounds good. I'll try it."

Jean walked a few feet back into the coffee kiosk and continued talking with me as she prepared my drink. It felt a little like asking her out on a date, but she was so warm and genuine; I was looking forward to getting to know her better.

"Are you accepting new clients at the moment?" I asked her.

She poured a big scoop of ice into a plastic cup. "I do have a couple openings for March."

I asked, "Can Brent and I take you out for lunch and see if we're a good fit?"

"That would be great. Let me give you my number." Jean pressed a button on the cash register that spit out some blank receipt paper. She ripped it off, grabbed a pen, and wrote her phone number down. She handed me the iced tea and her number, and I handed her my debit card. I took a sip of the drink. My stomach wasn't revolting for once.

The following weekend, Brent and I met Jean at a restaurant and sat on the patio under the shade of an umbrella. We ordered lunch and got to know each other a bit better. After a while, we opened up about our gender creative parenting plans.

I told Jean that Brent and I weren't going to assign a gender to the baby; we were going to use they/them pronouns and focus on raising a happy, healthy child without gender stereotypes.

Jean leaned forward in her chair and said, "I love that. I would absolutely love to be a part of your birth story, and I think it's wonderful that you aren't going to assign a gender."

"I'm glad to hear you're into it," I told her. "Now we just have to try and find a midwife who gets it."

I told Jean that we wanted to have a home birth. Not only did I love the idea of giving birth at home since being a part of the home births of two of my younger sisters; a home birth also appealed to me as a gender creative parent because there wouldn't be hospital staff buzzing around, and we wouldn't be in a labor and delivery unit that labels babies by binary gender. We would be in the comfort of our own home with a midwife and a doula, where Brent, Zoomer, and I could just bask in the lovey-doveyness of becoming a family.

"I know the perfect midwife for you." Jean smiled. "You need to meet Kathleen. But you need to call her, like, yesterday, because her schedule fills up quickly."

Jean gave me Kathleen's contact information, and as soon as I got home after lunch, I opened my laptop and sent an email to her. I let her know how far along I was and shared some information about our parenting philosophy. I told her we weren't going to assign a gender to our child, and I asked her if she had any availability. If so, would she be interested in taking us on?

I exhaled a huge sigh of relief when Kathleen got back to me and said she was interested. In fact, she was "intrigued" and said she'd love to meet us to see if we were all a good fit. I was trying to navigate my first pregnancy and gender creative parenting without any experience. It was terrifying to reach out to strangers and make myself vulnerable to the unpredictability of their responses. I was worried our family would be treated like a spectacle.

In my worst fears, I imagined a home birth assistant or a pediatric medical assistant learning about us as gender creative parents and feeling so strongly against our philosophy that they would tell people about us and blatantly disclose Zoomer's sex. I was afraid that people would somehow find me on social media or via my work email and harass me or talk to a local news reporter about me, and that reporter would be knocking down my door, demanding that we explain ourselves. I felt cautious and guarded, which was out of character for me. I didn't want to let too many people into our world during pregnancy and birth and the early days of parenting. I wanted to get my bearings.

I realized I was so concerned with the possibility of people getting hung up on the gender creative parenting aspect that I forgot to recognize that there are so many other things that they might be more concerned about, like where my placenta was and whether or not there was sugar in my urine. Kathleen didn't care that I didn't want to assign a gender to the baby; she just wanted to make sure that baby entered the world as safely as possible. Once we found our birth team, a feeling of calm came over me. I felt understood and safe and was able to have the pregnancy experience that I wanted, one in which Zoomer's genitals weren't important, gender assignments were nonexistent, and growing and birthing a healthy baby was the focus.

Kathleen was a great fit for our family. I showed up to her office on a late summer morning, and she answered the door barefoot. My prenatal visits felt more like visiting a favorite relative's house than a clinic. It was cozy. Kathleen took great care of me during my pregnancy, and she had an ultrasound machine and would let us sneak a peek at Zoomer during every appointment. We got to see Zoomer's legs kicking around and their little heart beating fast like hummingbird wings. Kathleen referred to Zoomer as "baby" and didn't use any gendered pronouns. Gender wasn't ever a topic; it was refreshing. I was so thrilled that Kathleen would be with me when I gave birth to Zoomer. Things were moving along beautifully.

SIX

The Talks

Once Brent and I decided to get pregnant, I began dipping my toes into what conversations about gender creative parenting were actually going to entail. I started with some low-hanging fruit. I had casual conversations about our decision to parent without assigning a gender with my best friend, Raye, and my graduate school adviser, Claudia. They were unfazed by my plans—we shared similar ideas about gender. I collected some easy wins.

I talked about gender creative parenting with my youngest sisters; they didn't bat an eye. I told my older brother and got a "You're weird, but I love you" response. I stood on a stage, teaching my gender and sexuality class with an audience of a hundred undergraduate students and made a case for why I thought gender creative parenting would become more mainstream and that I would do it if I ever had a baby.

The confidence wasn't constant, though. My trepidation about talking to my sister Mykenzie and to my parents surprised me. I was dreading the conversations.

What's wrong with you, Kyl? I'd scold myself. *Just bring it up the next time you talk to them!* I was trying to hype myself up, trying to find the courage to tell my sister that I was going to try to get pregnant, and

I wasn't going to assign a gender to my child. And I didn't have any resources, no guidelines for reassuring my family. I felt relatively confident gender creative parenting wasn't going to be a disaster, but I knew my sister and parents could have benefited from some proof.

Mykenzie has a young daughter. She and I had been talking more often now that I was thinking about getting pregnant, and I loved it. Mykenzie is hilarious and easygoing, and I looked forward to our weekly chats. I was nervous about telling her, though, *because* she is a mom. I, a not-yet-parent, had things to say about parenting, and I didn't want to offend her.

One afternoon, while on the phone with Mykenzie, I finally blurted it out: "I'm trying to get pregnant, and I just wanted to let you know that I'm not going to assign a gender to the baby." The phone line was quiet for a few seconds.

I could hear Mykenzie's daughter, Mara, cooing and playing with toys.

"OK," Mykenzie said.

"And I'm going to use *they* and *them* as pronouns for the baby instead of *she* or *he*. I want to create a space that is as free of gender stereotypes as possible for the baby to grow up in." Again, a couple of seconds of silence as she gathered her thoughts.

"I want to support you. As a parent, you get to do whatever you believe is best for your family." She sounded upset. "Do you think I'm wrong because I'm raising Mara as a girl?"

My heart sank.

"No, Mykenzie. You're a great mom, and Mara is wonderful, and you're doing everything that you feel is right for her. This is just what feels right for me and Brent." I continued, "I have learned so much from you about parenthood, and I know I will be a better mom because I have you as a role model."

I heard Mykenzie take a breath.

"What do I call the baby? What gender-neutral word can I use that's equivalent to *niece* or *nephew*?" she asked.

"Good question." While on the phone with her, I googled "gender-neutral term for niece nephew" and got an adorable search result. "Oh gosh, this is cute," I said. "*Nibling.* They are taking the *N* from *niece* and *nephew* and replacing the *S* in *sibling* to make *nibling.*"

"That is really cute," Mykenzie said. "I'll put my own spin on it; the baby can be my little niblet." We both laughed. *Niblet* was perfect.

Something that I hadn't considered was that my friends and family were my messengers. I only had to talk about gender creative parenting with one person, and then they would tell the people closest to them, and the message traveled through others. Mykenzie would talk to her husband, her husband's family, and our mutual friends whom she was closer with. People had the freedom to speak more uncensored thoughts than they probably would if I were the one talking with them about gender creative parenting. It saved us a lot of time as well as a lot of stress. I didn't feel the need to initiate every conversation. This was our decision, and I didn't need to be present for any and all potentially negative comments.

A few months later, I was pregnant and feeling frustrated that there weren't many publicly available, easily findable resources about gender creative parenting. I figured if I was wishing there was more information, others might be too, so I decided to make the resources I wanted. I hoped that, eventually, someone besides our own family and friends might find them helpful.

Brent and I created raisingzoomer.com. I taught a sociology of gender and sexuality class to university students for a living, and Brent made digital things look beautiful for a living. We figured we could combine our talents to make a simple website for our family and friends where we could try to explain our ideas about gender creative parenting that we thought were important.

Over the course of several months, I spent time writing short blog posts. I felt that sending family, friends, and coworkers a link to read on their own time would be easier than trying to find the perfect opportunity and forcing conversations about all the ins and outs of gender creative parenting. The mini-essays included posts like how to use they/them/their pronouns and the difference between sex and gender. I wanted to be accessible and try to meet people where they were. I wanted to share my perspective in a gentle, nonthreatening way. They could read it, process it, and then ask me some questions if they had any. I figured it would take some of the pressure off everyone, and I think it did.

Before I told my parents about my gender creative parenting plans, I was able to get in touch with the parents of Sasha and Storm, the kids I had read about in the news years before. In a brief email exchange with both of them, I asked, "Are you glad you parented this way?" And they both told me that yes, they were glad they parented this way, and they would do it again. I felt some camaraderie and comfort knowing that these parents had done it before me and felt that not assigning a gender was one of the best parenting decisions they ever made. I felt some relief.

During my second trimester, on the other side of the most unpredictable first twelve weeks, I decided it was time to tell my mom about my gender creative parenting plans. I had struggled to get excited about my pregnancy during the first trimester. Miscarriages are common; my mom had had several. I needed information and screenings and ultrasounds and time to put my mind at ease. With every passing week, I relaxed a little bit more. The embryo turned into the fetus turned into the maybe-baby, and then I started allowing myself to bond with Zoomer Coyote. I was ready to start seriously committing to gender creative parenting, and I needed to talk to my parents about it.

I called my mom and got through the initial small talk. Then I took a breath. "Mom, I want to talk to you about something. Is it an OK time?"

She responded, "Yes, what's up?"

"OK . . . well . . . I don't want to assign a gender to Zoomer," I said. "Meaning I don't want to call Zoomer a boy or a girl. I just want Zoomer to be a baby and a child without all the expectations and stereotypes that come with being a boy or a girl."

My mom said, "I'm not surprised that you would want to do that."

I breathed a little sigh of relief. "So there's more to it. I'm going to use the pronouns *they*, *them*, and *their* when referring to Zoomer, instead of *she* or *he*. If we're not using gendered pronouns, then people will be less likely to have gendered interactions with Zoomer. I know it might take some practice, but I want everyone to use these gender-neutral pronouns for Zoomer until they are old enough to tell us what pronouns they want us to use for them." I could sense my mom's brain processing it all.

"OK, but I will know Zoomer's gender, right?" she asked. We were entering a new level of discomfort.

"Mom, I want you to have a close relationship with Zoomer. And eventually, you will know their sex, but in the first couple of months, we aren't going to tell anyone Zoomer's sex. That way, everyone can get used to using they/them pronouns and be more conscious about just treating Zoomer like a baby."

I could tell she was a little upset. "I am a little shocked," she said. "I'm just trying to process this because it's so different than what I imagined grandparenthood to be. So I don't get to know Zoomer's gender?"

"Mom, I won't even know Zoomer's gender. That's part of this. I believe that Zoomer's gender is up to them, and they will tell us their gender identity and what pronouns they want us to use for them when they are ready. That will probably be in a few years, so in the grand scheme of things, it's not that long. We will let you change diapers and give baths to Zoomer when they are a few months old; we just want you to understand why we are doing what we are doing."

"Well, what are you going to do when you're at the park, and Zoomer wants to run around naked?" she asked.

I thought for a moment. "Oh well . . . did I run around the park naked a lot when I was a kid?"

We both chuckled. My mom said, "You know what I mean. How will you keep their body a secret?"

I understood what she meant and agreed it was a big question.

"I want Zoomer to feel positive about their body, and I guess if we need to change a diaper or into a swimsuit in public, we'll just do it. We'll cross all the bridges as we get to them. The main point is I want Zoomer to have the opportunity to discover who they are without labels and limitations and shame for crossing socially constructed boundaries, ya know?"

My mom took a breath, "I know, honey. So what do you call this?"

"I'm calling it gender creative parenting. I made a blog where I wrote some explanations. You can read it if you want; it might help this make more sense, and I want you to ask me any questions you have."

As we ended the call, she told me that she liked to think that she raised me to be a leader and inclusive and loving, so this made sense to her. I couldn't help but smile.

When it came to telling my dad, I worried that he wouldn't be completely honest with me. I knew if he disagreed with what I was doing, he probably wouldn't tell me, and if he needed clarification, he probably wouldn't ask for it. My dad doesn't like conflict, but I also didn't want him to harbor feelings of confusion. I often thought of him as my audience for the blog. He's a smart and curious person, and I figured if I included the right hyperlink on a blog post, I could direct him to corners of the internet that held information I wanted him to learn more about.

When I brought up gender creative parenting to him on the phone, I learned that one of my sisters had already told him about it.

"I don't understand it," my dad said.

I didn't really know what to say. He wasn't a nineteen-year-old student of mine. He was my dad, and I cared about what he thought, and I didn't want to disappoint him. While I was searching my brain for the right thing to say, he beat me to it.

"But I don't have to fully understand it to support you. I'm going to love my grandbaby, just like I love their mom."

My heart jumped into my throat. I thanked him and told him that I had made a website and written some blog posts to help him understand it a little bit better. And if he needed more explanation to please just ask me. I didn't want it to be hard on him.

The fact I was scared to tell my parents left Brent terrified. Brent is a worrier. He cares about what people think much more than I do. He knew his parents would be shocked. Brent has a wonderful relationship with his parents, but our geographical situation was already not ideal; we lived in different hemispheres, thousands of miles apart. Now a baby was on the way, the first grandchild, and not only were we on the other side of the world, Brent was about to throw a wrench in their grandparenting gears with this news.

A subtle cloud of anxiety surrounded him in the days leading up to telling his parents. He wanted to do it on his own. He wanted to show his parents that he was committed to gender creative parenting. I was glad for that. I already felt some guilt that I had taken their son from Australia. I was afraid they might feel that gender creative parenting was all my idea too.

Brent first told his siblings, Nathan and Kimberley, about our gender creative parenting plans. Both were on board immediately and incredibly supportive.

Finally, about a month before Zoomer was born, Brent announced that he was going to call his parents.

"I'm going to go in the backyard," he told me as he grabbed his cell phone.

"OK. Good luck." I didn't know what else to say. I knew this was going to be very difficult for him.

It was a February day, but sunny and relatively nice out. I was putting a basket of newly washed baby clothes into the dresser in the room that was soon to be Zoomer's when I heard the murmur of Brent's voice. I walked up to the window and saw Brent. He was pacing around, wearing a gray T-shirt and black Nike track pants, walking barefoot on the grass that wasn't quite green yet. He was holding his phone up to his ear with his left hand, and he dragged his right hand along the clothesline, where the rainbow of newborn onesies I was putting away had been drying an hour earlier. I watched him for a moment, observing his body language. He looked relaxed. I hoped it was going well, and I went back to tidying up the baby's room.

About five minutes later, I heard the back door close. Brent put his phone down on the kitchen counter and walked toward the living room.

"How did it go?" I asked him.

He sat down on the couch, and he was quiet for a moment. "It went OK. It's just a lot to ask of them. I think I should have talked to them about this sooner. It came out of left field for them, and I feel bad that I let my own anxieties delay the conversation. I should have been priming them for this since we started talking about having a baby."

Brent's feet were moving quickly, tapping the floor beneath him. He turned his head to the right, away from me. He was struggling. I wanted to help him. I wanted to help ease everyone's mind. But I was still trying to ease my own. I didn't really know what lay ahead for us.

I rubbed Brent's back. "I know what you mean, babe. I delayed the conversation too, which kind of backfired in a way, because our parents probably already had ideas in their head about this baby and were looking forward to either having a granddaughter or a grandson next month, and we asked them to backtrack and start over in imagining what grandparenthood was going to be like."

"I think they are just worried for us," he said, looking sad. "They don't understand why we want to take it to the point that we are. They think our life is going to be so much harder, and of course, they don't want us to get hurt."

"Is this making you have second thoughts?" I asked Brent.

"No. I want to do gender creative parenting. But I can want to parent this way and be scared too."

I nodded. Brent's anxiety wasn't really surprising to me. My anxiety, however, caught me more off guard. "I think we're doing the right thing," I said out loud. It wasn't for Brent as much as it was a statement of validation for myself. I did think we were doing the right thing. I hoped I was right.

SEVEN

Zwischen

During week twenty of my pregnancy, I felt Z kick for the first time. We were in Australia, visiting Brent's parents, and I was sitting on their red sofa when it happened. It was a pretty magical moment. I grabbed Brent's hand and pushed it against the right side of my stomach. The next day, I would grab my mother-in-law's hand and press it beneath my ribs. Zoomer didn't move too often, so I tried to share the infrequent moments with anyone who was around—even the airport staff in Fiji on our way home.

When we got back to Utah, at every prenatal appointment since the night of their first kick, Zoomer was in the same position—head up in the middle of my tummy, bum down near my pelvis, and feet right near their face—breech, breech, breech. Zoomer hadn't realized that we had returned to the Northern Hemisphere and thought they were in the right position, Brent joked.

At the beginning of my third trimester, whenever Kathleen peeked in on Zoomer with her ultrasound, she mentioned what we already knew: Zoomer was in a breech position. At my thirty-five-week appointment, I slid off the table, wiped the gel off my belly with a tissue, and pulled my pants up and over my tummy and my sweater down. Brent and I sat on a sofa in Kathleen's office across from her.

"So should we schedule a time for you to come bring the birthing pool over to our house?" I asked her.

"We need to get this baby turned around," she said, suddenly very serious. "In Utah, midwives aren't allowed to attend home births of babies they know are breech. I can't bring anything to your house until baby is head down."

"Oh," I said, feeling nervous. Brent squeezed my hand, and it dawned on me: *She's not confident Zoomer is going to turn.*

Kathleen looked me in the eyes and said, "You've got some homework to do. You need to go on spinningbabies.com and do all the moves they tell you to do. You should see a chiropractor and an acupuncturist; tell them you have a breech baby you hope to turn. You can try moxibustion. Do you have access to a pool?" she asked, and I nodded.

"Get in that pool," she prescribed. "I'm going to refer you to Phillip Young. He's a breech baby guru and does something called external cephalic version, or ECV. I think we need to get you in to see him."

For two weeks, my focus was on trying to get Zoomer to turn. I propped one end of our ironing board on our bed and climbed on, lying on my back with my head toward the floor and my feet above me on the bed. I waited. Nothing.

I saw a chiropractor three times. He was confident he could get Zoomer to turn through the magic of his adjustments. His adjustments weren't magical enough.

I saw an acupuncturist twice and got needles in my feet. There was a tennis ball involved, but no movement.

I ordered moxibustion sticks off the internet. I sat in my backyard on a periwinkle plastic chair, set the matching chair in front of me, and put my feet on it like an ottoman. I lit the ends of the moxibustion sticks with a lighter and rested a stick on each of the armrests. I positioned my feet so the moxibustion smoke was directed near my little toes. I sat there in a nightgown and a denim jacket in the early afternoon, tilted my head back, and basked in the first sunny day as winter was giving way to spring. The moxibustion smoke smelled like marijuana. I waited for a nosy neighbor to pop their head over the fence and for Zoomer to suddenly get the urge to turn. Neither happened.

I put cold gel packs on my stomach, hoping it would make Z uncomfortable, and they'd flip. Brent made me a Spotify playlist of songs that had "turning" or "flipping" lyrics that I listened to and sang along with, vigorously dancing in our kitchen. Zoomer was uninspired by the Byrds's "Turn! Turn! Turn!" And their little bum stayed put near my pelvis.

The day before I was scheduled for an attempted ECV with Dr. Young, I went to the indoor swimming pool at the University of Utah. While undergrads flirted in the hot tub and fit athletes swam fast laps, I waddled out in a mismatched bikini, stepped my swollen feet into the pool, and plopped under the water.

I was like a playful manatee, swimming and alternating front flips and backflips. Young college students watched as I played a solitary set of "hands up, stands up." After a half hour, tired, I heaved the bottom halves of my legs over the side of the pool, resting them on the wet, cold concrete. The rest of my body floated in the water.

"Zoomer," I said with water in my ears, my voice sounding different in my head. "Honey . . . I'm trying to get you to turn. I need your head in my pelvis and your tushy in my rib cage." My very pregnant belly buoyed me above the water.

"I really want to have a home birth, Z," I confessed. "I don't want to deal with the hospital. It's sterile and crowded, and I don't want them to gender you. I don't want to be treated like a weirdo on your birthday."

The time was ticking for Zoomer to flip. I was slowly admitting to myself that it was unlikely. I was reluctantly surrendering to the more likely reality—Z was going to be born via cesarean section, and that certainly wasn't taking place in my living room.

~

B rent and I walked into the labor and delivery triage clinic, and I approached the counter. It was time for the ECV.

A medical assistant walked into the waiting room and called out, "Christina?" I looked at Brent and rolled my eyes. Brent laughed. This happened all the time. When someone didn't know how to pronounce Kyl, they would just decide that I preferred to go by my middle name, Christina.

"It's Kyl," I said as I used the wooden armrests to push myself upright.

Brent stood up and held my hand. "Come on, Tina, let's go flip our baby."

We were brought into a labor and delivery room and I changed into a gown. I climbed onto the hospital bed, and the nurse placed a band around my belly that would monitor Zoomer's heart rate. Brent and I were left alone in the room.

"This feels very hospitally and busy . . . there's a lot going on in here!" I was taking in everything in the room—cabinets and monitors and curtains and a sofa and a big piece of equipment that was where a pediatric team would work on a newborn if necessary. "I don't want to give birth in here." As I said it, I realized I wouldn't be giving birth in this room. If I was giving birth in the hospital, it was going to be in an operating room, where I'd be grateful for all the equipment and bustle.

I could hear a nurse in the hallway fidgeting through a closet. They stopped and shouted to another nurse, "Oh no! We're out of girl beanies!"

I looked at Brent and sarcastically teased, "Oh no! There's no girl beanies? What the hell is a girl beanie?"

From the sofa, Brent chuckled. He was taking his powerlessness in this situation in stride. He reassured me: "We'll bring our own beanie, babelove."

I leaned back against the propped-up bed, and we basked in the ambient noise of the rhythmic swooshing of Zoomer's little heartbeat from the monitor.

A woman in her early thirties walked into the room and reached out her hand to shake mine. "Hi, I'm Dr. Amin," she said.

"Hi, I'm Kyl, and this is Brent." I gestured over to Brent, who was standing up from the couch and making his way to the side of the bed.

Dr. Amin looked over to Brent and smiled. "Hi, Brent." She returned her dark-brown eyes to me. "So you have a breech baby?" she asked.

"Yes, I do."

"Mind if I take a look?" she asked.

I gathered the blue-and-white gown in my hands and pulled it above my stomach.

Dr. Amin smiled when she saw my belly. "I can tell baby is breech just by looking at you, but we'll take a quick peek with the ultrasound to confirm."

She put some cold jelly on my abdomen. In Kathleen's office, the jelly was kept in a warmer. I had a running list in my head of the differences between Kathleen's office and the hospital, and Kathleen's office was winning by a landslide. Dr. Amin placed the ultrasound wand into the jelly, gently pressed down, and started moving the wand around until she could get a visual of Zoomer on the ultrasound screen. No one had mentioned where Dr. Young was or when he'd be coming. I had met Dr. Young just a few days before at the consultation appointment. He was kind and made me feel very comfortable. He had a great reputation, and I was hopeful that if anyone could flip my baby, it would be him. He was who I had been referred to and who I was hoping my care would be transferred to, if necessary, for the short remainder of my pregnancy.

Dr. Amin started touching my stomach with her hands and feeling for where Zoomer was and how she might manipulate them. It was obvious that she was going to be attempting to do an ECV.

I asked her, "Do you know when Dr. Young will be here? I was expecting him to do the procedure." She looked up at me. I could see in her eyes that she was disappointed I had asked and that she was about to respond to me the way she had responded hundreds of times before.

"I'm a doctor, and I have training to do this and am very experienced. Dr. Young will be here soon, but I am going to attempt this first." She wasn't upset with me. But I could tell that she must get asked a lot. A young woman of color, with light-brown skin, having to reassure a patient that she is, in fact, a doctor. I felt bad. I knew she was a doctor, and I hadn't assumed she wasn't a great doctor. I just wanted my doctor, the one I'd met seventy-two hours earlier.

Dr. Amin tried turning Zoomer for several minutes and wasn't having any luck. Dr. Young walked into the room, a little short of breath.

"Hi, sorry I'm late. I had to come from another hospital!" He reached over and shook my hand and then Brent's. The two doctors chatted ECV chat for a few seconds, and then Dr. Amin returned her hands to my stomach and tried to gently push Zoomer again. Nothing. After a few failed attempts from Dr. Amin, Dr. Young decided it was his turn to try.

Having an adult's fingers under my rib cage and pelvic bones isn't the best feeling I've experienced. I lay back on the bed looking up at the ceiling as Dr. Young tried to move Zoomer, and Brent and Dr. Amin watched. Brent said that Zoomer's head would move down a bit, but as soon as Dr. Young let go, Z's head would return right back to their usual spot, smack dab upright.

After several minutes, several different positions, several attempts on Dr. Young's end, and several deep breaths and an internal *It will be over soon* mantra on my end, Dr. Young removed his hands from my belly, stood up straight, and placed his hands on his hips. I looked at him and knew what I was about to hear.

"Well," he started, "I don't think this is going to work. I'm sorry." In that moment, I imagined he felt more disappointed than I did.

"You have a couple of options," he continued. "You can try for a vaginal birth. I think you're a good candidate for that, and I'd be happy to be here for you if that's what you choose, or you can schedule a cesarean section."

I took in my options and then asked, "About how many first timers attempt a breech birth vaginally but end up having a C-section?"

"About fifty percent," he answered.

I nodded slowly. I didn't love those odds. He said he'd give us a minute to think about it, and he left the room.

Brent held my hand. "Are you OK?" he asked.

"Yeah, I'm OK," I said. I was glad that we tried the ECV, but trying to turn Z had been exhausting, and I didn't want to do it anymore. "I feel like I can surrender to this and finally move forward."

There was a knock at the door, and then Dr. Young appeared. "So what do you think?" he asked, standing at the side of my bed with Brent on the other side.

"I want to schedule a C-section," I told him.

Dr. Young nodded. "OK. Your due date is the nineteenth? I'm going to be in Canada until that day. If you want to schedule a C-section for then or earlier, we can get you scheduled with my partner. But I, of course, would love to do this for you, and it's not likely you'll go into labor before then, so if you want to pick your baby's birthday and let me know, I'll get that scheduled for you." He wrote his cell phone number on his card and handed it over to me. Before leaving the room, he said, "Sorry I couldn't get baby to turn."

I took the gown off and changed back into my clothes. Brent and I walked to our car in the hospital parking garage.

"I'm hungry," I told Brent. I hadn't eaten all day; those were the instructions, just in case there was an emergency that called for an immediate cesarean section. Brent drove to a sandwich shop and went inside to grab us some late lunch. When he got back to the car, he found me sobbing.

He put the bag of food down and wrapped his arms around me. "It's going to be OK, babe."

"I just need one day. I'm just gonna be sad and disappointed today, and then I'll be fine." I wiped my tears from my cheeks with some napkins out of the bag, and we drove home and ate our sandwiches on the couch and watched *Seinfeld*.

I threw the wrappers away and then walked up to the big 2016 calendar we had on the wall. I scanned the month of March. Saturday, March 19, had a big circle drawn around it, with "due date" written inside it. I'd been fixated on March 19 since I was assigned to care about that date. I hadn't noticed that the next day, March 20, was the first day of spring. I smiled.

"Hey, Brent!" I shouted.

Brent walked into the kitchen. "Yeah?"

"What do you think about our kid's birthday being March 20, the first day of spring?"

He smiled. "I like that."

I nodded. "Me too. I'll see if Dr. Young can do it that day."

After a few texts with Dr. Young, he confirmed that while they usually don't schedule cesarean sections on the weekend, he had made a few calls and scheduled an operating room for that day. I grabbed a pen and wrote "Happy Birthday Zoomer" in the square of March 20. Then I whispered toward my belly, "Don't you dare try and come early!"

That night, I filled up the bathtub and poured an entire bag of Epsom salt in the stream of hot water coming from the faucet. I climbed in and soaked my sore body. I ached from the ECV. I ached from where twenty fingers had tried to manipulate Zoomer through parts of me, some bone, some muscle, some organs. I cried my last cry that I had allotted myself for this situation. I got it all out. I cried for the loss of the home birth I wanted so badly. I cried for the last month that had been so stressful and borne none of the results I had desperately tried for. I cried about the C-section that I would be having in sixteen days.

I cried because I would now also be recovering from a major surgery, in addition to being a new parent. I cried about having a baby in the hospital and all the unknowns of what that meant for me as a new gender creative parent.

That week I spent a lot of time online. I retired my home birth Pinterest board and fired up a cesarean one. Lounging on the couch one night, scrolling through cesarean info, I looked to Brent. "Well, the good news is I don't have to prep padsicles anymore." He nodded, not having any idea what padsicles were.

"I also get my first catheter!" I said, genuinely excited.

As the countdown to Zoomer's birthday began, I loosened up. My doula, Jean, and her business partner, Elle, came over and played out a mock cesarean section with Brent and me in our living room. I lay down on the rug; Jean played anesthesiologist, then switched roles to obstetrician. Elle described what the operating room would look like and where Brent would stand. My nerves began to calm.

~

A week before Zoomer was born, every box on my list was checked. My hospital bag was packed. All Zoomer's clothes had been washed and put away. The car seat base had been installed in the car. Brent and I had tidied and deep cleaned the house. I had all the essentials that one needs to bring a baby home (which isn't much). I was ready, I guess, but I was feeling odd. I was weepy. I sobbed during an Arby's commercial.

I kept thinking, *This is the last time I do* this *before I'm a parent* while doing mundane stuff, like changing the toilet paper roll. I was fascinated when I bought things with an expiration date when Zoomer would be here. "I'm buying this yogurt while I'm pregnant, but I'll eat it as a parent. Whoa." And then tears ran down my face in the grocery store, and I laughed at myself as I wiped them away. Those fortieth-week hormones were a trip.

I was sitting on the couch one afternoon, watching TV, distracting myself from all the feelings raging through my body. I was days away from meeting my baby. My phone buzzed. Jean, my lovely doula and now close friend, sent me a link to an article. "I'm thinking of you today and thought you might be needing this." I clicked the link and was directed to an online article, "The Last Days of Pregnancy: A Place of In-Between," by Jana Studelska.[18]

I started reading the essay. Jana described exactly how I was feeling, in between two lives, in a state of *zwischen*. Parenting itself was intimidating—terrifying even, in an exciting way. Gender creative parenting felt even scarier. I was twenty-nine and looking forward to becoming Zoomer's mom. I felt confident that I was going to be an awesome parent, but I was scared for what my life was going to look like as a gender creative parent. I didn't personally know anyone who had done this—only Sasha's and Storm's parents, and they were mostly private about it all.

Up until now, when people asked me, "What are you having?" I could say, "We're going to wait and be surprised." There was no confusion or follow-up. With Zoomer inside my womb, the protective layers of my body, skin, and muscle guarded us from further questioning. In a few days, that wouldn't work as my go-to answer. People were going to inevitably ask, looking at me as if I hadn't understood the question, and repeat it: "Is it a boy or a girl?" and I wouldn't know how to answer. I genuinely would not know if Zoomer was a boy or a girl, or neither or both, until they told me. Would I feel like I was fighting some kind of battle every single day?

I was basking in the final calm moments before walking into what I assumed would be a relentless storm. I was bracing for arguments, for the gossip, the endless demands for explanation. My life was about to change dramatically, twice, at the same moment—as I crossed over from this child-free life of mine, where I was only responsible for myself, to a life of parenthood and a choice to alter childhood gender socialization for my child and maybe hundreds or thousands of others. I felt like a circus performer crawling into a cannon for the first time: terrified, not knowing exactly where I'd land or if I'd come out of this unscathed, but sure I wanted to do it.

~

I waddled for miles in the days before Zoomer was born. Contrary to what other pregnant people are wishing for at forty weeks, I wasn't trying to get labor started. My scheduled cesarean section would be on Sunday, and I was politely reminding Zoomer every morning, "Don't get any ideas. You had your chance for the birth canal, but that ship has sailed. Stay put till they cut you out." I just wanted as much fresh air as I could get before the whirlwind of new parenthood and surgery recovery was upon me.

I walked to This Is the Place Heritage Park. History has it that, on the land there, Brigham Young looked down on the Salt Lake Valley, declared "This is the place," and instructed the Mormon pioneers who had fled religious persecution in the Midwest and eastern United States to build their homes and make a life for themselves in this valley. I didn't have Mormon pioneer ancestry, but I could relate to the idea of trying to find a better, safer place for your children.

I got a boost of courage to be a gender creative parent. I knew there would be people who would support me. I imagined there would also be thousands of people who would rally around the message I was try-ing to send—kids deserve an opportunity to just be kids and to make their own way to a gender identity that feels right for them.

~

You can't eat or drink before a C-section. The concern is that you'll puke during the surgery and choke on your own yarf. I'm an eater and easily become hangry, so fasting isn't really my thing. If I wasn't allowed to eat or drink after 9:00 p.m. on the nineteenth, then I was going to eat and drink whatever I wanted up until 8:59. I pitched the idea of strolling to Manoli's, a Greek restaurant a couple of miles away, on Zoomer's birthday eve. Brent walked; I waddled, zigging and zagging through city blocks.

The walk was a mild emotional roller coaster. Brent and I hadn't made a concrete decision yet about how we were going to navigate gender creative parenting in the hospital the next day. There were really only two choices: (1) let Zoomer be gendered during our hospital stay, or (2) advocate for ourselves as gender creative parents. On one block, I thought, *A baby is going to be literally pulled out of a cut in my stomach tomorrow, and I'm trying to keep it together as it is, and I am worried about lobbing another thing into the mix, like policing people's use of pronouns. Zoomer won't be aware of what's going on, so we don't need to correct people for the three days we're in the hospital.* But the thought of Zoomer being gendered for three days made me cringe.

By the next block, my mind had changed. *Nope! It's a privilege of mine as a cisgender person to be able to go with the flow. I should make the harder choice to proactively make sure the birth team knows we are gender creative parents and that we use they/them pronouns for Zoomer. Too many transgender, intersex, and nonbinary people have to deal with this on a daily basis, and more cisgender people have to step up to make change.*

By the time we got to Liberty Park, just three blocks from the restaurant, I was physically exhausted, mentally drained, and emotionally depleted. Brent was feeling slightly anxious because I was the one who was supposed to be oozing confidence and making convincing cases for decisions. A big decision had yet to be made. I asked Brent if we could sit down at a nearby picnic table. I traced the diamond pattern in the metal tabletop with my swollen index finger and took a few deep breaths, as deep as I could take with a baby using my lung as a pillow.

"I'm going to make a decision before I stand up," I declared.

After a couple more breaths, I brought my eyes up to meet Brent's and said, "I think we need to do what we feel is right. And I feel like the right thing to do is stand our ground and stay committed to gender creative parenting, even when it's scary."

Brent nodded and added, "I'm struggling with the unknown. I'm already stressed about the fact we are going to be parents tomorrow. And in addition to just being a dad, I want to get gender creative parenting right." We both sat at the table as the sun set and the sky turned a deep navy blue.

Brent said, "But remember we aren't making a decision right now. The decision has been made. Tomorrow is the first time we are going to officially experience the effects of our decision."

We attempted to smile at each other. A smile of solidarity between our tiny team of two.

"Let's get you some food." Brent held out his hand and helped me off the bench.

We walked to Manoli's and ordered more food than we needed. We celebrated our final night as the Courtney-Myers duo. Tomorrow, we'd be a trio.

We took a cab home after dinner, and I drafted an email to Dr. Young. I briefly explained our gender creative parenting philosophy. I told him we would not be assigning a gender; we would be using gender-neutral pronouns, and I asked him not to disclose or make a big deal out of Zoomer's genitals. I added the link to raisingzoomer.com, the blog we'd made for our family, friends, and colleagues to help explain what we were doing, if he felt inclined to learn more. My finger hovered over the "Send" button a little longer than usual. I was nervous. A bunch of butterflies somersaulted in my stomach as I finally pressed "Send." Our gender creative parenting adventure had officially begun.

EIGHT

Happy Birthday, Zoomer!

Dear Family and Friends,

They say it takes a village to raise a child . . .

We are delighted to announce the arrival of the newest member to our village.

Zoomer Coyote Courtney-Myers was born on Sunday, March 20th, 2016, at 1:16 pm.

Weight: 7 Pounds 13 Ounces. Length: 19¾ Inches.

We have decided that instead of assigning a gender to Zoomer we want to go the gender creative route. We want Zoomer to experience all types of things and be free to explore and play with gender. It's likely that Zoomer will gravitate toward a gender identity in a few years.

We use the gender-neutral pronouns "they, them, their" and we also use "Z" as a substitute for words like he/she, him/her, his/hers. It takes a little bit of time to get used to, but we're confident it will be second nature to you soon.

To help you better understand the concept of and rationale behind gender creative parenting, we have written short articles and created a website for our friends and family. Also on the website is a link to a Pinterest page where we have compiled news stories and TED talks that help explain some reasons for gender creative parenting.

The website is www.raisingzoomer.com.

In the event that you do know what Zoomer's reproductive anatomy is, we kindly ask that you keep the information to yourself and continue using gender-neutral pronouns and words when referring to them and interact with them in a gender creative way—but if you slip up, don't be hard on yourself.

We know this may come as a bit of a shock to you—and we are happy to answer any questions that you may have. You can e-mail or call us anytime.

We are so excited to introduce you to Zoomer soon. They will be an even cooler kid because they get to interact with you!

Warmly,

Brent & Kyl

We emailed the birth announcement to our friends, family, and coworkers the day after Zoomer was born, and our inboxes filled up with an outpouring of congratulatory messages and love.

Whenever I think of Zoomer's birth story, I smile because it's a good story.

Dr. Young had told us to expect to be at the hospital around 9:00 a.m. on Sunday morning but that someone would call and give us the green light. I woke up early, around 6:00, too excited and nervous to sleep. I double-checked that I had everything in my bag, which was on the floor next to the soon-to-be-in-use car seat, and then sat on the couch for most of the morning, trying to distract myself on social media and watching TV, waiting for the hospital to call and tell us they were ready.

We finally got the call around 9:30 a.m. "Hi, Kyl. We're ready for you; come on up," said the person on the other end of the line. Brent and I got in the car and drove to the hospital, where we were greeted at the labor and delivery desk by a nurse.

"Hi. Having a baby today?" they said.

"That's the plan!" I responded.

"Do you know what you're having?"

It was the last time I got to say it with Zoomer still inside my body: "We're going to be surprised."

The nurse smiled. "That's exciting! Let me introduce you to Allison. She'll be taking care of you this morning."

Allison was in her early forties, with dark-brown, shoulder-length hair, half of which was pulled back in a ponytail. Fringe swooped across her forehead. She was wearing a white scrub top and black pants. "Hi, I'm Allison. It's nice to meet you. Let's get you to your room."

We walked into the room, and Allison handed me a gown. "Thanks," I said as I put my bag down and took the gown from her hands.

"I'll be back in a few minutes," she said, and she closed the door behind her. Brent sat on the couch. I had been here a couple of weeks ago. I knew the drill. I took off my shoes, sweatpants, cardigan, and T-shirt and slipped into the blue-and-white gown. I climbed up on the hospital bed and texted Jean. She wanted to come hang out with us and provide moral support during the wait, so I let her know our room number and that she could come anytime. She told me she was on her way.

Allison entered the room to insert an IV into my arm, which was surprisingly quite painful and would turn out to be the most pain I would experience that day.

"So you're going to be surprised, I hear," she said with a smile as she shoved a needle into a vein in my arm and held it in place with tape on my skin.

"Well . . . ," I started as I winced through the discomfort, "I know what the baby's sex chromosomes are. So I have an idea what their genitals might look like, if that's the surprise you are asking about . . . but I'm not going to assign a gender. I'm not going to call the baby a girl or a boy; I'm just going to let them be a baby. It was a little easier to say we're going to be surprised than go into that explanation at the nurses' station."

A look came across her face, not of confusion, not of understanding, just a look that she was processing what I had told her. A neutral "Huh" came out of her mouth. "I've never heard of that before. That's cool." Then she said she was going to go get me some ice water.

Allison returned with a big plastic hospital mug with a lid and a straw on top. It was filled with tiny pellet ice cubes and water.

"Here you go," she said as she set it down on the little table next to the bed.

"Thanks, Allison." I grabbed the mug and took a sip.

"Can I get you anything else right now?" she asked.

I brought the straw down from my lips. "Actually, I have a question. Can you tell me what types of things we will be getting for the baby here that are typically based on gender? Like . . . is there an identification card that is going to be on the little plastic bassinet while we're here?"

Allison nodded. "Yes, there will be a little information card with your last name on it that's on the bassinet. There's a blue card for boys and a pink one for girls."

I sat for a brief moment, then asked, "So what do you do for intersex kids? Or people who don't want to do the binary gender thing? Is there a green card lying around somewhere that we could use?"

Allison pondered my question for a few seconds. "There aren't any other cards. It's a good question. I don't know what we would do for an intersex baby." After a few seconds, she continued, "I don't know why we even use different cards for boys and girls; it's kind of silly when you think about it."

My eyebrows lifted up a bit. Maybe I had just planted a little gender creative seed in this charge nurse's mind.

Around noon, Dr. Young came into the room and smiled. He shook my hand and said, "I got your email. I promise we'll be very discreet about the bottom bits and respect your wishes."

I felt a weight lift off my shoulders. I was being validated. This wasn't weirding him out (to the point he showed it). He trusted me and was respecting my wishes as a gender creative parent.

I smiled and said, "Thanks for not treating me like I'm weird, Phil."

He smiled back and said, "I've had a lot of requests from parents in my day. This one isn't weirding me out."

A little before 1:00 p.m., after a quick ultrasound check to make sure Zoomer was in fact still breech—it could not have been more obvious with that noggin protruding out from under my ribs—it was time to head to the operating room. Allison handed Brent a pair of scrubs to change into and gave me a cap to cover my hair. Brent and I walked to the entry of the operating room, just a short stroll down the hall, and I gave Brent a smooch before a temporary goodbye; he had to wait in our room until they were ready for him.

An anesthesiologist and a couple of nurses were in the OR waiting for me. The room was white and bright and medical and sterile. The anesthesiologist approached me and introduced himself.

"Hi, I'm Lane. I'll be your anesthesiologist today."

"I was planning on having an unmedicated birth," I said with a straight face. A moment of silence passed, and I laughed. "Just kidding. Put all the drugs in me."

Lane chuckled, relieved, and helped me get up onto the operating table and administered the anesthetic near my spine.

I lay down, my back pressed against the table, as the drugs quickly got to work. He asked how I felt, and as the lower half of my body seemed to disappear, I excitedly admitted, "Not pregnant! It's great!"

Lane told me to let him know if I felt any discomfort at all, then sat down on a stool to the right of me, near my head, and looked at me with smiling blue eyes. He said, "I hear we are welcoming a free spirit into the world today."

I blinked a few times as I registered that he knew. "Yes," I said. "And I can't wait to meet them."

"What's their name?" he asked.

"Zoomer Coyote."

His eyes smiled again. "That's a perfect name."

There was a split second of calmness, and then the operating room was buzzing with organized chaos. Dr. Young and an obstetrics resident walked in; a pediatric team walked in; Brent was accompanied in. When I saw Brent, my heart started beating faster, and my eyes welled up with happy-nervous tears. He sat down on a stool to the left of me. "Hi, sweetie," he said. "How are you feeling? Are you feeling ready?"

I nodded. "I'm so ready to meet Zoomer."

Brent's eyes got a little watery. He squeezed my hand and said, "Me too."

A scheduled cesarean-section birth is surprisingly quick. I was looking up at the white ceiling. I couldn't feel what was happening; I couldn't see what was happening. So I just listened. I heard Dr. Young say, "Here we go!" and then the room was quiet.

Zoomer's cry pierced through the silence and entered my ears. The sound of their cry rewired my brain and embedded itself into every fiber of my heart. How could a sound I'd never heard before be so familiar? I looked at Brent and told him, "Go."

Brent stood up, walked behind the drape, and spoke to me from across the room. "Kyl, they're beautiful. They have a bunch of hair."

I smiled. I knew in a matter of seconds Zoomer would be in my arms, and I'd finally be able to lay eyes on this little human who had grown inside my body, a child I already had a limitless love for.

Brent brought Zoomer to me and helped situate them on my chest. Zoomer was swaddled in a blanket and had a beanie on their head. Their fresh neonate, blue-gray eyes were taking me in for the first time, and they scanned my face as I spoke to them. "Hello, Zoomer. Happy birthday, honey. I'm Kyl. I'm your mommy, and I am absolutely delighted to finally meet you." Zoomer's feet came right up to my mouth; they were breech in utero, and the pose stuck.

Brent was sitting next to me, leaning into us, with one arm around Zoomer and one arm around me. Our little family of three. Lane asked Brent if he had brought his phone in. Brent pulled his iPhone out of his pocket and handed it over to him. The sweet anesthesiologist, now with his mask below his chin, said, "Smile!" as he took a photo of us.

"You're the highest-paid birth photographer that there's ever been," I joked. I was oblivious to the fact that my body was being stitched back together. The only thing that mattered was happening on this side of the drape.

While we were in our love-drenched recovery in the hospital, the nurses from the labor and delivery ward informed the nurses in the postpartum unit about us, Zoomer, and gender-neutral pronouns. As shifts changed, nurses informed the next nurse who would be caring for us. Some nurses had greater ease using gender-neutral pronouns than others, and whenever anyone "slipped" (which was rare) and apologized, we said, "Please don't feel bad; we appreciate you trying!"

Over the course of our three-day stay, we interacted with dozens of staff, doctors, residents, lactation specialists, nurses, and nursing assistants, and everyone—and I mean everyone—was respectful and professional and gave it their best efforts, and not one person questioned our request.

The day after Zoomer was born, two pediatricians checked Zoomer out in our room: Dr. Davis, a supervising faculty member, and Dr. Patel, a resident. After looking Zoomer over, doing standard hearing and vision tests, and checking Zoomer for hip dysplasia after being breech for so long, Dr. Patel asked us who our pediatrician would be. Finding a pediatrician had been a task that was weighing on me—I wanted to find someone who would be respectful of our gender creative parenting approach, but we were also in a weird limbo period of health insurance plans, so we hadn't decided on anyone, which I told Dr. Patel. I had been afraid that pediatricians would think we were too radical and not want to take Zoomer on as a patient because they wouldn't want to deal with Brent and me.

"I'd really like to be Zoomer's pediatrician," said Dr. Patel. "I'm on board with your parenting philosophy." I was sitting upright in the hospital bed. I looked to Brent, and we smiled at each other. I turned and looked at Dr. Patel and said, "That would be great."

There are only a few things that could have made our hospital stay dreamier. I wish there hadn't been a sex-based, color-coded, gender-assuming card on Zoomer's bassinet. The card said "Baby Myers" on it, and its sole purpose was to easily identify a newborn, in the case they were in the nursery and not with a caregiver. Zoomer was in Brent's or my arms 90 percent of the time, so we didn't pay much attention to the bassinet. If I had known about the card ahead of time or if I was having another baby, I would be more proactive and creative and ask for a copy of the card, get one printed in a different color, and bring it with me to put on the bassinet myself. I can't remember what the beanie looked like that was put on Zoomer in the OR immediately after they were born. My eyes never left their eyes once they were given to me. They could have been wearing a chef's hat for all I know. When we got back to our room, within the hour Z was born, Brent put a simple white beanie on them that we had brought from home.

On Tuesday morning, I looked over toward our hospital room window, where the sunlight was pouring in. Under the window, on the small sofa bed, Brent was lying on his side, curled up, with two-day-new Zoomer in the crook of his arm. Both of them were fast asleep. As I filled out Zoomer's birth certificate form, my pen hovered over the options of "Male" or "Female" for a few seconds. There was no intersex option or unknown option or nonbinary option. I appreciated that at least Utah used the correct terminology. The "Male" and "Female" boxes were next to the prompt "Sex" and not "Gender." I did know what Zoomer's sex chromosomes were, and I had seen their genitals, which were typical for those sex chromosomes. As a population health sociologist, I am grateful that sex is a variable that is collected through birth certificates. It helps us see if there are imbalances in sex ratios at birth and helps us monitor sex differences in infant mortality rates. But I also recognize that assigning and documenting binary sex in this particular way harms transgender, nonbinary, and intersex people.

I filled in the box next to the sex marker that correlated with Zoomer's sex chromosomes and genitals and acknowledged I might not be getting it right. Zoomer needed a birth certificate so they could have a social security number and a passport and so that we had proof that linked them to Brent and me as their parents. Their birth certificate wouldn't be seen by anyone except those who were handling these official identification requests, so it wouldn't influence how Zoomer was being treated on a daily basis while they were a child. I decided that if Zoomer wants to change the sex marker on their birth certificate when they get older, then I will pay all the fees and support them in that process. Thankfully, Utah is a state where this will likely be possible.

It was, dare I say, easy to do gender creative parenting at the hospital, which was undoubtedly influenced by the privileges Brent and I have as a White, middle-class, insured, straight-appearing couple at a hospital in a progressive city. The medical staff treated us like it was no big deal and consciously used they/them pronouns for Zoomer. We had found a pediatrician who wanted Zoomer as a patient. It was a litmus test of sorts. With every interaction we had with a new person, my anxieties about what this new life would bring started to evaporate.

Giving birth in a hospital put my convictions through a test. If I was going to be a gender creative parent and put myself out there as a resource for other gender creative parents and an advocate for change, then I couldn't just talk the talk; I needed to walk the walk. Even if that walk was painful and resulted in a scar above my pubic bone and the need for Percocet to get through the first two weeks of parenthood.

A few weeks after we got home from the hospital, I was organizing some paperwork. I found a printout of a medical chart from when Zoomer was born, and at the top of our charts was the line "Parents would like their child to be treated gender neutrally." Someone had made sure that was one of the first things any nurse or doctor read before they came into our room and interacted with us. Believe you me, I did an ugly-happy cry at our kitchen table when I discovered that note.

While I had wanted to be in the tiny percentage of people birthing at home, Zoomer wanted to be in the tiny percentage of babies who are breech on their birthday. Zoomer taught me early that kids don't always turn out the way parents assume they will. What an appropriate lesson for a gender creative parent.

NINE

The Early Days

I surrendered to the oxytocin flooding my body, and Zoomer became my main priority. I didn't have to go back to work until June 1, so for eleven weeks, all day and all night long, my only responsibility was bonding with and caring for my beautiful newborn baby.

Our days consisted of me snuggling with and staring at Zoomer for hours, changing blowout diapers, and obsessing over the app I downloaded that tracked how often Zoomer was nursing and from which boob. The first week was especially hard because I struggled to stand and walk as I healed from the surgery. When Zoomer was a week old, in an ambitious move, I decided I wanted to walk to Coffee Stop.

Brent got Zoomer changed and wore them in a Solly Baby wrap. My mom was visiting and helped me out the door, and we started strolling down the sidewalk. "I'm feeling great!" I declared after the first block. "Isn't the human body amazing?" We got to Coffee Stop, ordered drinks, and started making our way back to the house when some external force opened me up, took my batteries out, and chucked them in the road. With each step, I experienced more pain, and I crouched in an effort to compress my guts, which I was just sure were going to spill out of my healing incision at any moment. I saw a bus stop bench twenty feet away, slowly made my way over to it, sat down, and said, "I'll just hang out here for a while."

Brent and my mom knew I wasn't going to make it back to the house three blocks away unassisted. I had overdone it, and to make it back to my bed I needed narcotics, a car, or preferably both. My mom, Brent, and Zoomer went home, and my mom looked after Z while Brent got in the car and came to retrieve me. I felt like I had been disqualified as a "Did not finish" in the six-block fun run.

Brent pulled into the driveway and looked at me. "You don't have to do everything. You can slow down. Everyone wants to help you slow down, but you have to give yourself the permission to do so." It was like telling a fish not to swim, and he knew it. But I tried to take his advice to heart, and I started asking for more help.

During the first month, we had visitors nearly every day, and my family rotated staying a few days with us. Brent or I would change Zoomer's diaper before a visitor came over or behind the closed door of Z's room. It wasn't a big deal. If Zoomer wasn't attached to my nipple, they were usually being held by Brent, one of their grandparents, or another family member or friend. No one in our social circle knew what Zoomer's genitals looked like. Everyone either called Zoomer by their name or used gender-neutral pronouns.

We didn't talk much about gender creative parenting in the beginning with our visitors. Everyone had gotten the birth announcement or had had a conversation with us before Zoomer was born. There wasn't much else to discuss regarding gender. We focused on other things. We talked about how perfectly spherical Zoomer's skull was since their head hadn't been smooshed in my unused birth canal and how it was difficult to try to nap during the day when Zoomer slept. We talked about how online search engines are a gift and a curse for parents these days. People oohed and aahed over the brand-new baby in their arms. "Their tiny fingernails!" "They have your nostrils, Kyl." "Oop! I think there's a poop in their britches!" "It's my turn to hold them now!" "How is feeding them going?" Everyone was simply falling in love with Zoomer and wanting to support us.

When Zoomer was two weeks old, Brent had to go back to work. The company Brent worked for gave him one week off, unpaid. Brent asked to work from home the second week, and his supervisor relented but expected him back at work the following Monday. Over the next few weeks, the visits from friends and family slowed down. Adjusting to life with a newborn was all consuming, and new parenthood started feeling lonely and isolating.

The days and nights all blended into each other during the first two months. I would nurse Zoomer, burp Zoomer, play with Zoomer, change Zoomer, swaddle Zoomer, snuggle Zoomer, get Zoomer to sleep, check Zoomer is breathing, find something to eat that required minimal preparation, check Zoomer is breathing, read the breast pump instructions, pump for twenty minutes, put a minuscule amount of milk in the fridge and sanitize pump thingamabobs, check Zoomer is breathing, turn on shower, swear I hear crying, turn shower off and peek head out of shower curtain, no crying, turn shower back on, swear I hear crying again, decide to wash hair later, get out and check on Zoomer, who is fast asleep, put on only pair of sweatpants that fit, now Zoomer is crying, and repeat.

The idea of having to go anywhere seemed overwhelming, but I also didn't want to be home all the time. Going to Target to get fingernail clippers was a half-day outing. I would need to bring thirteen diapers, four packages of wipes, and nine outfits, just in case. I'd put Zoomer in the car seat, drive to Target, take Zoomer out of the car seat, nurse Zoomer in the back seat, change a blowout diaper, change their clothes that were victims of the blow out, put Zoomer in the baby carrier, walk into Target. Forget what I'm there for. Wander for forty-five minutes because Zoomer is asleep, and there's no way I'm waking them up. *Fingernail clippers!* Go get the clippers. Walking to the checkout, I'd pass a parent with four kids and stop them to ask if they were a sorcerer because I simply could not understand how they could get four kids into Target, let alone keep them alive.

I scrolled through Instagram in the middle of the night while I nursed Z. During the hours that blurred late and early, I was certain I was the only person awake for miles. I'd look at people's photos and think, *It must be nice to have the energy to wash your hair* and *It must be nice to have time to eat something other than a cold piece of bread.* It was during one of the late-night nursing sessions that I created the @raisingzoomer Instagram account. I wanted to connect with other people who were doing gender creative parenting, in some way or another. I started searching hashtags, looking for community.

~

One afternoon, a month after Zoomer was born, Brent got home from work, put his bag down, gave me a kiss, and scooped Zoomer up.

"How was work?" I asked him.

"Overall, it was good. I had a stressful moment, though. I got in the elevator, and one of the executives was in it. He knew that I had a new baby at home, and he asked me if I had a boy or a girl. It made me feel panicky. I said, 'We're doing something called gender creative parenting. We didn't assign a gender. My baby's name is Zoomer.' And he just looked at me with this forced smile and blank eyes. And I knew he was probably thinking, 'What the hell is going on?' I was so relieved when the elevator doors opened and he got out."

We were silent for a couple of moments. Brent was standing, lightly rocking Zoomer. He looked down at Zoomer, who was falling asleep.

He continued, "Don't get me wrong. I'm so glad we're doing gender creative parenting. But it's like we don't get to experience the same amount of carefree joy in public as most parents because we're constantly waiting for the 'Boy or girl?' question. I wonder if people are talking about me at work. I mean, I know they are talking about me at work."

I felt my body temperature rise and my heartbeat speed up. The hair on the back of my neck bristled.

"At least you get to go to work and have intellectually stimulating conversations with people and go out for lunch and coffee every day. Oh, and you've managed to get dressed today," I snarled.

Brent looked down at Zoomer, who was now asleep. He calmly turned and walked out of the living room and down the hall and gently placed Zoomer down in their crib. He walked back into the living room and sat on the couch next to me.

"Kyl, I wish I could be at home with you and Zoomer. I wish I worked for a company with a family leave policy. I wish we could afford for me to say, 'No thanks, work, I'll be back when I'm good and ready.' But I don't. I have to go to work. I'm so grateful that you're home with Zoomer, and you are doing such a great job. You should take more time for yourself and make more plans for nights and weekends, when I'm here and can take care of Zoomer."

I felt embarrassed that I was upset with him. I felt guilty that I wanted time away from all these new responsibilities. I felt glad that Brent was finding himself in situations where he had to talk about gender creative parenting without me. I felt sad that gender creative parenting made us more nervous around strangers.

"It's just a lot," I admitted.

Brent was showing Zoomer the schools of colorful fish in the aquarium in the waiting area at Dr. Patel's pediatric clinic before Zoomer's two-month checkup. I sat in a chair, filling out some paperwork the receptionist had handed to me on a clipboard. The questions were about me. After eight weeks of questions about Zoomer's well-being, someone was asking me how I was feeling. It didn't say "Postpartum Depression Screening Tool" at the top of the document, but I knew what it was, and I answered all the questions honestly and gave it back to the receptionist.

While I was holding a newly immunized Zoomer, Dr. Patel said, "I'm a little concerned about the answers you gave on the questionnaire. Your score indicates you might be at risk of or experiencing postpartum depression. How are you feeling?"

I took a breath before answering. "I love Zoomer, and I'm loving being a parent, which I know is not in question, but parenting is bananas. I have a baby attached to my nipples sixteen hours a day. I don't get a lot of intellectually stimulating interaction most days. I'm exhausted. I'm nervous about going back to work in a few weeks. I totally have a splash of postpartum depression. I don't know how any new parent wouldn't." Suddenly I couldn't stop talking. "I'm not overly concerned about it; I don't want to harm myself or Zoomer. I'm just trying to figure out my new reality, and I know I'm going to be fine eventually, but this is hard. I'm confident it's going to be OK, but I want to feel like I have a grasp on my own identity, and I don't right now." Brent put his hand on my knee and gave me a reassuring squeeze.

Dr. Patel nodded. "Parenting is tough. You are doing a great job, and Zoomer is so happy and healthy and lucky to have you two as parents."

Equally shared parenting is difficult in the beginning if one parent is at home more with the baby. Brent and I were determined to get into a groove so parenting felt balanced and fair, and so my transition back into work would be as easy as possible. Sure, I was home alone with Zoomer from 9:00 a.m. to 5:00 p.m. the first two and a half months of their life, but Brent was home more than he wasn't and equally involved in parenting from 5:00 p.m. to 9:00 a.m. and all in on the weekends. I found myself trying to make sense of the space I was existing in between biology and society.

I was a mammal who had just given birth and committed myself to the responsibilities of caring for an infant, and I was also a woman in a relationship with a man in 2016. I reminded myself to hold back when Zoomer cried so Brent had a chance to respond to them. I restrained myself from trying to micromanage every caretaking interaction, not necessarily overriding a maternal instinct as much as my control-freak instinct. Brent was a human parent with oxytocin coursing through his veins too. He was drawn to caring for and bonding with Zoomer just as much as I was. I wanted Brent to be an empowered dad, and that meant he needed to have opportunities to become empowered.

My Mormon upbringing and status as the second oldest of five kids meant I had more experience taking care of kids than Brent did. But in regard to Zoomer, Brent reminded me, "You may have more experience than me taking care of kids, but you don't have more experience than me when it comes to this kid." I had the advantage of learning Zoomer's cues and being in charge of creating their schedule because I was at home with them during the day. In the evening, I would talk with Brent about what I thought was working, teach him the tricks, and get his input.

I taught Brent how to swaddle.

"I fold this down like this, put Zoomer on it, wrap one side over their body and tuck it under them, then I bring the other side around, and then I bring the bottom part up and tuck it into the top like that, and voilà, a snoozy Zoomie burrito."

Brent was eager to learn what I found was working, and he shared with me what he thought was working, and when we were both stumped, we turned to Google.

We had discussions and came up with the routine; we both knew how to make bottles and change diapers and give baths and get Zoomer to sleep. We established a rule: unless Zoomer's safety was a concern, we kept our mouths shut about how the other parent did things. If the end result was a fed, clean, sleeping baby, then it didn't really matter how you got there. Tomato, tomahto.

When Zoomer was seven weeks old, a friend invited me out for drinks. "Do you mind if I go to the bar tonight with Shireen?" I asked Brent over the phone while he was at work.

"Not at all. Go for it," Brent said.

When Brent got home, I got ready to go out. I nursed Zoomer, and I drove to the bar, where I had two tequila and sodas and caught up with my friend for three hours. During the entire course of the night, I didn't check my phone once. I knew Brent was completely capable of caring for Zoomer.

When it came to diapers, Brent changed more diapers at nighttime because I changed diapers during the day when Brent was at work. Once I went back to work, we'd alternate. "It's your turn," one of us would usually say after describing the terrible poopy diaper we had to change earlier. Sometimes we'd play Rock, Paper, Scissors to determine who was up next on diaper duty. After Zoomer turned one, Brent no longer let me play the "But I had to be pregnant and have a baby cut out of me" card when I was trying to guilt him into changing diapers when it was my turn.

It can feel nearly impossible to find an equal parenting balance when one parent is the baby's food source (especially if breast- or chest-feeding).[19] I breastfed Zoomer for four months. During the month before I went back to work, I pumped every day, hoping to build up a stock of milk in the freezer, but my output wasn't very impressive. My mental health was fragile in the early days when I wasn't getting much sleep. Both Brent and I had to get at least six hours of sleep to be able to function at work (and be somewhat nice to each other), so we began to sleep train Zoomer.

Brent and I decided to introduce formula when Zoomer was about eight weeks old. That way, we knew Zoomer could get enough to eat during the day, and it would take the pressure off me as the sole food source. The first time I gave Zoomer a bottle with formula in it, they drank it down like it was the most delicious thing they'd ever tasted. I stood in the kitchen, half-sad that they hadn't refused it and half-elated that other people could now share the stress of keeping Zoomer alive.

For Brent and me, equally shared parenting is one of the most important aspects of gender creative parenting. We both wanted to work and earn money, and we both wanted to contribute equally to household and parenting responsibilities like cooking and cleaning and caring for Zoomer. If we wanted our child to grow up to believe that all genders are equally capable, then we needed to show that to them in our home. Constantly and consciously, Brent and I discussed how we could dismantle gender norms in our partnership because the protective shell was about to crack. The fourth trimester was over, and the world was about to start having an influence on Zoomer.

TEN

New Encounters

I realized quickly that, unfortunately, the younger a child is, the more people ask if they are a boy or a girl. Those early months were a double whammy. I was trying to find my groove as a parent and my confidence in gender creative parenting. Hands down, my biggest anxieties about gender creative parenting were related to having to talk about it with someone for the first time. Yet I didn't have as many conversations about gender creative parenting with strangers as I thought I would. And I realized that talking about gender creative parenting was like working a muscle. The more I did it, the easier it got.

The overwhelming majority of the time, someone (cashier, flight attendant, nice stranger at the park) would see Zoomer, assume a gender based on their clothes, and say something like, "How old is she?" or "He's so cute." To which I would respond, "Ten weeks." Or "Thanks." Conversation over. I wasn't stopping every friendly grocery store clerk and saying, "Well, actually, we use gender-neutral pronouns." Once Zoomer is older and lets me know what pronouns to use for them, I'll stop and correct people all day long if they misgender Zoomer. But in the first few months, I did not have the bandwidth to discuss pronouns in the produce section every time I was buying bananas.

If the person was someone who would probably be interacting with Zoomer quite a bit, like a barista at a café we frequent, then I would say something like, "We don't know Zoomer's gender yet, so we use they/them pronouns for now." And more often than not, the barista would say, "That's rad. So nice to meet you, little Zoomer."

When Z was almost four weeks old, Brent, Zooms, and I went to the Winter Farmer's Market in downtown Salt Lake. As we walked into the historic repurposed train station, we were met with smells of freshly baked bread, brewing coffee, and a "Hey, guys!" from Giselle, a friend of a friend. Zoomer was fast asleep on my chest in a baby wrap, and Giselle leaned in to look at them. I had only met her a couple of times before, but we followed each other on Instagram. She put her hand on Zoomer's back and looked up at Brent and me with a huge smile on her face. "I just can't get my brain around what you two are doing. I'm just dying to know! I was talking to my friends about you guys, and I was like, 'I just want to take all Zoomer's clothes off so I can know!'"

I looked at Brent, speechless.

Brent put his hand on my back and looked at Giselle. "Um. That's a weird thing to say."

Giselle laughed. She was completely unaware of how uncomfortable she had made us feel. She readjusted her canvas tote bag on her shoulder, smiled at us one last time, said goodbye, and walked away.

"Wow, I did not handle that well," Brent said.

"Don't feel bad. I didn't say anything! Now I feel like I can't change Zoomer's diaper in the public bathroom here because I'm afraid she's going to be tracking me, just waiting for an opportunity to see Zoomer's genitals. That was gross and weird and inappropriate, right?"

"On so many levels." Brent was shaking his head in disbelief. "I feel like I should have done more to shut her down and help her see how messed up that was."

I took a big breath. Zoomer was still asleep. I tried to shake off the invasive feelings.

Zoomer was about seven weeks old when my sister-in-law, Kimberley, came to visit us from Australia. We decided we'd go on a big, important trip to Costco, to get some essentials—you know, a twelve-pack of toothpaste and a hundred-pack of string cheese. Zoomer was in their car seat that attached to the stroller; the car seat and stroller each had a canopy that closed together, so you couldn't see Zoomer at all.

I left Kimberley with the stroller and cart in the main corridor and walked down an aisle to grab a vat of peanut butter. As I reached to grab a container, I heard, "Is that a boy or a girl in there?" My body remained facing the floor-to-ceiling shelves of spreads, my head slowly turned to the right, toward Kimberley and Zoomer. I saw a person standing next to Kimberley and the black capsule on wheels that contained my precious Zoomer.

Kimberley looked at me with wide eyes and an expression that read "Help." My eyelids narrowed, and I'm sure my hazel irises were eclipsed by dilated pupils. "Is that a guy or a girl in there?" he pressed Kimberley again. People had asked if Zoomer was a boy or a girl before, but not as aggressively or incessantly as this person was. You couldn't even see Zoomer. I could have had a shih tzu puppy in the stroller. I felt protective because someone was asking Kimberley about Z's gender. I didn't want Kimberley to feel the stresses of the question like we had been for the last two months.

My steps became bigger, faster. I'd believe it if someone said they saw steam coming out of my nostrils. Kimberley couldn't have moved the stroller and the cart by herself, and the man asked her the question one more time as Kimberley said, "I don't know. Here's their mom."

I looked at the man, who was probably in his early seventies—my height, with a flannel shirt tucked into jeans and a rodeo-style belt buckle. Let's call him Herb. Herb had a trucker hat on his head and had no idea his well-intentioned question came off as an interrogation I wish he hadn't initiated. He looked relieved that I had arrived, like he could finally know if this infant who he couldn't even see had a penis or a vulva. For the fourth time in forty seconds, he asked, "You got a guy or a girl in there?"

I looked at him and asked, "Why does it matter?"

He stood there, looking at me, confused. As Kimberley and I turned to escape, someone said, "Come on, Dad," and our parties went opposite ways. I turned to watch them walk down the aisle with sliced fruit in cans the size of car engines.

Herb had a six-foot tree in his cart. It was spring, after all, and Costco does have fabulous deals on seasonal foliage. To avoid running into Herb again, I tracked that tree during the remaining fifteen minutes of our time in Costco. I would look for branches and leaves bobbing above the aisles, like the bright-green plumb bob that floats above the Sims characters. I knew where Herb was at all times. "We need bread. Oh, Herb's over there; let's go get laundry detergent first."

Zoomer woke up and started cooing, grunting, and stretching like a newly hatched velociraptor. I opened the canopy to say hello. I was greeted by their tiny, cute face and a not-so-cute stench. I asked Kimberley if she would mind taking Z out to the car for a diaper change. I'd go pay for everything and be out shortly. I stood in the checkout line, and Herb and his adult child got in line at another cashier's stand. I looked at Herb. Herb looked at me. I finished up at the checkout and started walking out of Costco, about ten yards behind Herb and that tree. We left the store at the same time and were parked in the same aisle directly across from each other. I see my car, with the back hatch door up, and Kimberley changing Z's diaper. My kid's ass is exposed to the Costco parking lot, and Herb, the baby-gender police, is about to walk right by. Kimberley saw Herb coming and now holds the Guinness World Record for quickest diaper change. Kimberley buckled Z into their seat and got into the car.

I didn't want Herb to have the satisfaction of seeing Zoomer's genitals and feeling like he knew what my child's gender must be. It's not that I was angry at Herb; I was angry at the cultural norm that Herb was a proxy for. I was annoyed that a stranger would literally yell at me, "You got a guy or a girl in there?" multiple times, like anything about my family was any of his business.

I watched Herb as I got to the car, making sure he stayed on his side of the aisle as I found space for a case of La Croix. He watched me play Tetris with boxes. Before I got into the driver's seat, I took one last look at Herb. He was looking at me and gave me a little nod, and I did the same. *Good luck with your tree*, I thought.

When Zoomer was four months old, Brent, Zoomer, and I flew to Seattle, where I was presenting some of my dissertation research at a conference. From the Seattle airport, we got on the light rail to head to our hotel downtown. I was wearing Zoomer in an Ergobaby carrier. They were facing outward, so their back was to my chest. I was holding on to the pole in the middle of the train car, and an elderly person started making cute, silly faces with Zoomer. Zoomer was giggling and kicking their legs in appreciation of this fun new friend. The person looked up at me and asked, "Boy or girl?"

I took notice of the seven other strangers around me on the train who were also about to hear this little explanation I was about to give to this sweet senior Seattleite. Brent grinned at me as if to say, "I'm so ready to watch this."

"Well . . . ," I started, "this is Zoomer. We didn't assign a gender. We're going to let them decide if they are a boy or a girl or something else." I paused. That was probably enough for now. I looked at our new friend, who was slowly nodding, processing what I said.

"Well, good luck with that!" they responded.

"Thanks!" I said.

At the next stop, they made a final funny face at Zoomer, said, "Bye, Zoomer!" and slowly got off the train with some assistance from their cane.

I like to think that for every thirty seconds of an awkward conversation about gender creative parenting I have with a stranger, I might be preventing Zoomer from experiencing half a dozen stereotyping remarks or gendered microaggressions. And I might be gently nudging a stranger in the direction of thinking twice about how much power they allow gender to have in their interactions with kids in the future.

In a restaurant once, as we waited for a table, someone looked over at me holding tiny Zoomer; they smiled and said, "Boy or girl?" I gave the gender creative parenting elevator pitch, and their face lit up after processing it. They said, "That's great! Sorry I asked. It's such a habit, and I need to break it. My sister's kid is nonbinary, and it's been great learning about that. How old is your baby? Mine are seven and nine now, not so baby." I told them Zoomer was five months old, and we talked about the adjustment of parenthood and how time flies.

As I got more confident, the little gut clench that would happen inside me whenever someone asked, "Boy or girl?" started to loosen. I knew I was doing the right thing for my family, and every day, I got a little more well versed in talking about it. I figured out which lines worked best for describing gender creative parenting and kept it short and sweet. I could zap any awkwardness by pivoting to a parenting-related topic that wasn't about gender, giving them an out. Something like "I saw your kid riding a balance bike. We aren't close to bike-riding age yet, but they seem like a great way to get kids comfortable on a bike. Does your kid like it?" If the person wanted to talk about gender creative parenting, I was here for it, but I tried to show them, *Look how much we can talk about without relying on gender as a guide.* I wanted folks to leave having had a positive interaction with a gender creative parent.

The first time I felt the "Please don't ask me if I have kids" feeling, Brent and I were at a wedding, and three-month-old Zoomer was at home with a babysitter. Brent and I sat down on the white chairs in a green field up Millcreek Canyon, waiting for the ceremony to begin. The couple to my right started chatting with us. They told us how their kids were friends with Melissa, the bride. Then they talked about how they were so excited for their kids to have kids. A voice inside my head said, "Girl, you are ten seconds away from being asked if you've given your parents grandbabies yet. Get out of this right now."

I blurted out, "There's moose up here! I wonder if we'll see one!"

Everyone looked at me, the couple and Brent looked at each other, all of them thinking, *Is she having a stroke?*

As we walked toward the reception after the ceremony, I told Brent, "I just did not want to talk about gender creative parenting right then." By then, I had noticed that it's easier to talk about it when Zoomer is actually with us, and people can see a cute kid who is happy and has a personality and an adorable face.

Brent put his arm around me. "Don't feel bad, Kyl. Being a parent and doing gender creative parenting isn't your whole identity. It's totally OK to not want to talk about it." He pulled me closer as we walked up to the bar to order a drink. "Your moose pivot was weird, though. So work on that."

Later that night, as we danced at the reception, the newlyweds, Melissa and Ryan, were making their rounds. We clinked our glasses and gave the couple a congratulatory hug. Melissa, my friend, a children's ICU nurse, kept her hand on my arm. "Kyl, I just wanted to let you know that the way you are raising Zoomer has had such a positive influence on me. I realized I was using different adjectives to describe my patients. I'd call the boys tough and strong superheroes, and I'd usually call the girls beautiful little princesses. I realized that these are sick kids who need space to be sad and scared about what they're going through and also need to feel brave and like they can fight and heal. So I'm doing better with that now. Just trying to give the kids whatever they might need in the moment and not any useless gender stereotypes."

I was so touched. "Thanks for telling me that, Melissa. Those kids are lucky to have you!"

"Zoomer is lucky to have you!" she said. We hugged again, and the newlyweds carried on celebrating.

While there have been a few occasions, like at the wedding, when I was simply not in the mood to discuss gender creative parenting, most of the time, I'm like any other parent, happy to have a chat about my child.

I was on a flight from Salt Lake City to Denver for the Society of Family Planning's annual meeting. Brent and Zoomer would have a great time together without me for five days, as they often did whenever I traveled for work. I found my aisle seat, next to a fifty-something-year-old woman sitting by the window. I sat down, said, "Hi," and pulled out my book to read. As we were taking off, my eyes wandered to her reading material. It was a magazine published by the Church of Jesus Christ of Latter-day Saints, and the article she was reading was about how husbands and wives should both be involved in household finances. I started reading it out of the corner of my eye and then lost all sense of the privacy she deserved and turned my head toward her lap so I could continue reading the article more comfortably. She looked at me.

"Sorry, I didn't mean to be a nosy creep. I just noticed your article, and I am really into personal finance stuff . . . and I'm happy to see that kind of article in a Mormon publication."

She smiled. "It's OK. You can read it after I'm done if you want."

I smiled back. "Thanks. I think I got the gist."

She put the magazine down and asked me, "Are you a member?"

"I used to be," I said. "I resigned my membership a while ago. The Church doctrine doesn't really align with my values. But if it aligns with yours, I'm happy for you." Ever the pivoter, I asked her, "So where are you headed today?"

"I'm going to see my son and daughter-in-law and my new grandbaby in Massachusetts."

"Oh, that's exciting! I bet they'll be so glad to have you around!" I said, genuinely happy for her.

"I haven't made it out there yet, and my grandbaby is almost one," she confided.

"I know how you're feeling. My baby is eight months old, and we are flying to Australia next month so they can finally meet their grandparents in person. We're all excited about it!"

"*They*? Do you have twins?" she asked.

"No. Just one. We didn't assign a gender, so we use gender-neutral pronouns," I said, confidently. I had eight months of gender creative parenting muscle flexing. We were only twenty minutes into a ninety-five-minute flight. I had to have been feeling confident to dive into this conversation with someone I literally could not get away from.

She slowly nodded. I had come to know that nod well. It's the "I'm processing the words you just told me and figuring out which one of my eighty-six questions I should ask first" nod.

With conviction, she told me, "I believe that gender is something that is given to us by our Heavenly Father before we even come to our families on Earth and that there are only two genders. We have preordained roles as man and woman."

I smiled at her. "You are certainly entitled to your beliefs. I personally know quite a few people who experience gender outside the man-woman binary and so many people who feel constrained by the binary. I like to think that if there is a God, then God is thrilled with how diverse and beautifully complex the human experience is. And I'm down for the Golden Rule of treating people how you want to be treated, so I choose to treat everyone with love and acceptance and respect." I shrugged and took a sip of my ginger ale.

She smiled at me, and we were both quiet for a moment. She didn't press me any further on the gender creative parenting front.

"Do you want my pretzels?" she asked.

"I absolutely want your pretzels. Thank you."

We went on to have a long conversation, Janet and me. She told me that I needed to have at least three children, and her primary reason was that if one dies, at least you'll still have two. I laughed out loud and told her I thought that was a terrible reason to have three children, and I was quite happy with one for now.

She told me that she was worried about leaving her seventeen-year-old daughter at home in Salt Lake, fearing she would get into trouble with boys, which is why she had delayed visiting her son and grandbaby for so long. I asked her if she talked honestly about sex with her daughter. Horrified, she said, "Absolutely not." I encouraged her to reconsider when she got home and told her she might be surprised at how beneficial those conversations could be for both her and her daughter.

We landed in Denver and waited for every other passenger to deplane. I got up and grabbed my luggage and hers from the overhead bin. We walked up the aisle and through the jet bridge together and out into the terminal. "Well, Janet. It was nice meeting you," I told her.

"You too, Kyl. Thanks for your advice about talking to my daughter about you-know-what. And good luck with the no-gender baby thing."

I chuckled. "Thanks." And we went our separate ways.

ELEVEN

Kid-Land

It may not be like this everywhere, but in Salt Lake City, Utah, long waiting lists at high-quality childcare centers are a thing. Like, "Get on a waiting list as soon as you find out you're pregnant! Hell—as soon as you start *trying* to become pregnant!" kind of thing. I knew this about Salt Lake, but it hadn't been a concern of mine because I was planning on being at home and using occasional sitters until I got a job offer the following year. Originally, my plan was to try to find some childcare help through the LGBTQ resource center at the university or through the gender studies student listserv.

I had accepted a job much sooner than I expected, which was going to start a few months after Zoomer was born. Brent already worked full time, and we didn't have childcare. Our closest family member was 302 miles away, our farthest, 8,166. We were in a bit of a pickle.

I knew about Kid-Land, a daycare center a few blocks from our house. I had nannied some children who went there and had been inside a few times. I liked the staff, I liked the vibe, and I liked that it was a ten-minute walk away. One morning in March, about a week before Zoomer was born, I waddled over to Kid-Land. I entered the front office and was met by a friendly smile belonging to Robin, the director. She told me that there was an eight-month waiting list.

I walked closer to her desk and leaned an elbow on it.

"I'm gonna be real with you, Robin. This daycare is a ten-minute walk from my house. I have known people who have come here, and they loved it, and I don't want to go all over town getting my name on lists. I want to be here, and if it's November, so be it, but I'm going to schmooze you all spring and all summer and figure out a way to move my name up that list."

She smiled. "I like you."

"I like you too."

"So, do you know what you're having?" Robin asked.

I put a hand on my round belly. "Well, I'm confident it's a human baby. I know I'm naming the baby Zoomer. I have a little information about Zoomer's chromosomes and anatomy, but I'm not going to assign a gender based on that. I'm going to do this thing called gender creative parenting. We use they/them pronouns instead of she/her or he/him pronouns. I don't want Zoomer to be treated like a stereotypical girl or boy and only offered half the world. I just want Zoomer to get to be a kid. I think they'll find their gender identity in their own time."

Robin smiled, a genuine one, complete with smiling eyes. "I like that. There are several kids here who don't conform to typical gender norms, and we support them. We try really hard to just treat the kids like kids. We call everyone 'friends' instead of boys and girls, and we create an environment where kids can try all sorts of things. I think this will be a good fit."

Now I was smiling. "Thanks for being so cool about all of this."

"It makes sense," she said.

I filled out the application—leaving the gender question blank—and wrote a check for the waiting list fee. I said goodbye to Robin and left Kid-Land with an awkward, hugely pregnant skip. I called Brent on my walk home. "Babe! The director of Kid-Land was so great!"

If you're on a waiting list for childcare, let the schmoozing begin! Every month, we brought a new treat. Cookies from Ruby Snap, cupcakes from the Sweet Tooth Fairy, doughnuts from Banbury Cross. "Hi . . . just me, Zoomer's mom. Just wanted to pop in to let you know that this is still the only list we are on, and we're excited to bring Zoomer here! Your new haircut looks great! Enjoy the cookies! Byeeeee!" Brent took the next month's schmooze shift. We'd bring Zoomer in for added bonus points because they were so damn cute; we were confident that every glimpse someone got of them improved our chances of being moved up the list.

It was June 1 and my first day at my new job. We had to figure out something creative for the in-between time while we waited to get in at Kid-Land. The week I started my job, Brent took the week off work and stayed home with Zoomer. My friend Liv helped us out a few days a week during the summer. Liv was also a sociology graduate student and had a flexible summer schedule and a need for some cash. It was a perfect match. Liv is a badass vegan queer powerhouse of environmental feminist magic, and I was stoked that Zoomer would be basking in their presence. Liv watched Zoomer Mondays, Wednesdays, and Fridays when I went to work, and I "worked from home" on Tuesdays and Thursdays. That means I did the best I could to check my email during Zoomer's naps. In hindsight, I cackle at the assumption I was going to be able to write a dissertation at home with a baby.

Brent would leave work early as often as he could to get home and care for Zoomer. I took Zoomer to work a few times and set up a little baby-friendly area on the floor next to my desk. During a weekly all-staff meeting, Zoomer was in the middle of the circle of chairs, lying on a blanket. Their arms would uncoordinatedly flail their ball across the room, and whoever was closest would grab it and roll it back to Zoomer, without skipping a beat in finishing their sentence.

People were being as supportive as they possibly could be, but I was looking forward to being able to commit to my job without the distractions of an adorable infant cooing on my lap as I tried to study the ins and outs of Medicaid family planning waivers. In July, Robin called me and said, "Hi, Kyl, we have a spot for little Zoomer starting at the end of August." *Hallelujah!* You would have thought I had just won the lottery. It felt like it. I was stoked!

On the day Brent and I dropped Zoomer off for the first time, we walked into Kid-Land, and Robin was at her desk, smiling. She greeted us with a welcoming hello, and she taught us how to check Zoomer in and out each day.

Robin said, "I was registering Zoomer in our system this morning, and the form asked for a gender. I left it blank, and it let me proceed without putting anything in. I thought that was pretty cool!"

I smiled. "That is cool! Thanks for doing that, Robin." Knowing Zoomer was in a place where our parenting decisions were respected and supported made dropping Zoomer off a little easier.

That first day, Brent and I stayed for a while in the nursery. The nursery had three caretakers: Ann, Lupe, and Revati. I sat on the floor with Zoomer and talked with the caretakers for about fifteen minutes. I told them what gender creative parenting meant to us—that we didn't want Zoomer being treated one way or another just because of their anatomy. We wanted Zoomer to just be treated like a baby and offered all types of toys and read all sorts of books and described with all sorts of adjectives. We wanted Zoomer to be snuggled and wrestled. We told the caretakers about gender-neutral pronouns and gave examples for how to use *they/them/their* in the singular. We let them know about our blog, where they could learn more. We reassured the teachers that we understood it can take some time to get used to and that we appreciated their efforts and asked them not to be hard on themselves if they slipped up. We encouraged the teachers to ask us any questions they had; we were happy to answer them.

Whether or not the caretakers understood or agreed with gender creative parenting, they treated us with respect, and it was obvious that they were consciously trying to engage with Zoomer in a gender creative way. Getting used to they/them pronouns took a little bit more time, but not long, maybe a month or so. The staff at Kid-Land were committed to getting the hang of using they/them pronouns for Zoomer, and the language change happened quickly because they made the effort to do so.

In the infant room, every month they did an art project with the babies using their feet. It was ridiculously cute. In September we got a little masterpiece—Zoomer's foot as a corn on the cob. In October we got a foot-ghost. Just the cutest little keepsakes of my baby's tiny footsies.

A few months after Zoomer started at Kid-Land, one of their teachers, Lupe, and I had a conversation when I came to pick Z up. She said, "Today I was doing an art project with the babies. And I got out pink paint for the girls and blue paint for the boys, and then I stopped and thought, *What am I doing? I'm just going to use the same color paint for all the babies.*" She said she was trying to break the habits that come from a lifetime of being taught to treat babies differently based on gender. Needless to say, I was grateful that the people who were taking care of Zoomer every day were committed to checking their own biases and trying to pivot their actions to create an environment where children aren't categorized and treated differently based on their anatomy.

When Zoomer was about ten months old, I rocked up to Kid-Land to pick them up. I was a little caught off guard, because Ann, Lupe, and Revati weren't in the room. Instead, there were two substitute caretakers. The substitutes were using gendered pronouns, and one tried to play matchmaker with Zoomer and another baby, based on gendered assumptions.

I know I'm lucky that it took ten months before someone played cupid with my kid. I know some marriages are often jokingly arranged in utero. But I didn't like it.

I tried to be cool, ignoring the implied message and responding with a kind smile. "Every baby is Zoomer's friend." I scooped Zoomer up, and we went home. A few days later, I had a conversation with Robin. We had a productive discussion about how I don't want people making assumptions about Zoomer's future sexuality, and I don't think it's a good idea to sexualize babies. Robin totally agreed and apologized that it had happened. She said they would figure out a way to bring it up in the next staff training without shaming the teacher. Robin wanted to make sure Kid-Land was an inclusive space and pump the brakes on binary gender stereotypes and sexualizing. Robin also decided she wanted to make sure all the staff knew what gender creative parenting was, in case they ever interacted with Zoomer. From then on, I noticed whenever there was a substitute in Z's class, they were referring to Zoomer using gender-neutral pronouns.

When Zoomer turned two, they were moved up with some of their friends to a class for older kids. I knew Zoomer would be in a class with kids who didn't know them yet, and we'd be seeing a lot more of some new parents. Inspired by a post in the Parenting Theybies Facebook group from my fellow gender creative parenting friend Leah, I created "hello cards" to introduce our family to the other families. I got some cute little cards with elephants on them, and I bought little pots of Play-Doh for each of the kids in Zoomer's classroom. Inside the card, I wrote this message:

> Hi! We're Zoomer's parents, Brent and Kyl. We wanted to introduce ourselves to you because Zoomer is now in the same class with Ruby! Just so you are aware, we are gender creative parents and we use they/them/their pronouns for Zoomer. You can visit our blog raising-zoomer.com or text us if you ever have any questions about it. We look forward to getting to know you better and we know Z is excited to Play-Dohgether with Ruby!—Warmly, Kyl & Brent

In the weeks after I left the hello cards in the kids' cubbies, several parents stopped me in the hall or the parking lot to say hi and thank me for the note. They told me how they thought gender creative parenting was great and tried to challenge gender stereotypes in their own homes and with their extended families. We started giving each other book recommendations and inviting each other to birthday parties and playdates. We're a little community there—all of us thirty-something-year-olds, trying to have careers and raise kind humans. I'm glad to be doing it with all of them.

During the first three years of Zoomer's life, gender wasn't really a central focus at school. For the first two years, the kids could barely talk. As they all approached their third birthdays, they talked way more about dinosaurs, finger paint, and whose toot was loudest than anything gender related. I don't hear many of the kids talking about gender too much yet, and the way they use gendered pronouns is all over the place, and no one really has pronouns dialed in yet. The beautiful thing, though, is *they* is in the mix with *she* and *he* because the teachers want to help Zoomer feel welcome while also teaching the other children the importance of gender-neutral pronouns and words. Zoomer comes home from school, climbs onto my bed, and starts jumping and singing a song they learned in class. "Five little monkeys jumping on the bed; one fell off and bonked their head!"

Of course, gender is a part of Zoomer's life at Kid-Land. The majority of the staff are cisgender. Every child besides Zoomer was assigned a gender at birth. I hear Zoomer get called all sorts of pronouns by other kids, sometimes *she*, sometimes *he*, sometimes *they*, but most of the time *Zoomer* (although in toddler speak it sounds like *Thoomer* or *Dooma*). I hear parents and teachers sometimes say phrases to other kids like "You're such a big boy!" or "What a brave girl!"

I imagine a teacher has slipped before and called Zoomer a gendered term, like *boy* or *girl*. Judging from how quickly teachers correct themselves when they accidently use a gendered pronoun for Zoomer,

I bet they quickly find a gender creative replacement. What matters is how consciously and intentionally I see Zoomer's teachers try to interact with Zoomer and all the other kids in a gender creative way. The teachers compliment the boys with the painted fingernails and never discourage them from grabbing the plastic high-heel pumps out of the dress-up box. Teachers encourage the girls to ride the bikes fast and don't stop them from getting muddy, and when a girl pulls the Spider-Man costume out of the dress-up box, the teachers thank her after she rescues them from a pretend monster. All the children receive copious amounts of cuddles and attention when they are hurting . . . either from scraped knees, upset tummies, or missing their parents.

I make sure to spend time with the kids in Zoomer's classroom, trying to make whatever positive impression on them that I can. I roar and chase them in the gym until I'm out of breath and collapse on the floor, where the kids pile on top of me and yell, "Wake up, lion!"

I sit down on the floor in the classroom, and three-year-old Naomi brings me a book. I read *If You Give a Moose a Muffin* and replace the pronouns with *they/them/their*, just to sprinkle some gender neutrality into story time.

Daniel gives me a big hug whenever I come to the class, and I thank him for being such an amazing hugger and friend to Zoom.

Galen looks me up and down and comments on my fabulous blush-pink jumpsuit. "Why are you wearing pajamas?" Galen asks.

I laugh out loud and say, "Galen, this fabulous article of clothing is called a jumpsuit. I am about to go to work, where I am a boss, and it is important to me to look like a snazzy leader *and* feel comfortable." The teachers laugh, and so do the kids.

"Zoomer's mommy wear pajamas to work." Savannah laughs.

I joke with the kids as I leave the classroom. "Listen, Savannah, that's Dr. Myers to you, and any of you can borrow this jumpsuit when you're a boss." Savannah laughs.

"Have a good day, friends!" I say as I blow them all a kiss and close the door behind me to head to work in my boss-pajamas.

Just a few weeks shy of Zoomer's third birthday, I got the weekly update email from Kid-Land. In it, parents were told that the Kid-Land staff would be using the ASQ-3 developmental screening checklist for all the kids in their care. The questionnaire is from Ages and Stages and is used to measure how children are developing in areas like speech, physical ability, social skills, and problem-solving. It's meant to identify a child's strengths as well as any areas where they may need some support. I remember completing an ASQ-3 questionnaire at one of Zoomer's well-child checkups. It asked questions like, "When a loud noise occurs, does your baby turn to see where the sound came from?" Then the response options included yes, sometimes, and not yet. Nothing on the early questionnaires had anything to do with sex or gender that I could remember. When I got the email from Kid-Land, though, I made a mental note to myself to ask if there were any questions related to gender on the thirty-six-month questionnaire before they screened Zoomer.

A couple of hours after reading the email, I drove in an afternoon snowstorm to Kid-Land to pick Zoomer up. I walked into the office to clock Zoomer out, shaking the snowflakes off my coat. Robin was at her desk.

She smiled at me and said, "I saw Zoomer's outfit today! They picked that out all on their own?"

I laughed. "Oh, did you like the 'two shirts and the shorts over the leggings' look? They are such a ham. But they have their own style, and they rock it!"

Robin and I started talking about the ASQ-3 questionnaire.

"There's a question about gender on it," Robin said. "It directs the staff to ask the child, 'Are you a boy or a girl?' and I just wanted to let you know that we aren't going to ask that question to Zoomer."

My hand reflexively went up to my heart.

"I appreciate that. My guess is Zoomer would either say 'I'm Zoomie!' or 'I'm three!' I haven't even heard them use the words *boy* or *girl*, let alone identify as one."

Robin smiled and told me that she didn't think the question should be asked of any of the kids, even the ones who were assigned a gender or had identified with a gender, so they weren't going to ask it. They didn't believe the question means anything for kids' development, and they did not want to perpetuate the idea that there are only two gender options. Robin had reached out to Ages and Stages to petition them to remove the question and found out there was already a movement against it, and it wouldn't be included in the next edition.

I walked out of the office and toward Zoomer's classroom with an ear-to-ear grin on my face and feeling like I was roller skating on clouds. I opened the door to Z's class, and Zoomer came running over to me, yelling "Mommieeeeeee!" with arms wide open, ready for a big hug. I gathered them in my arms and gave them a kiss.

Zoomer ran over to their teacher, Abby, and gave her legs a hug. "You come over to my house for coffee, OK, Abby?"

Abby laughed. "Oh, I forgot to tell you, Kyl. Zoomer has invited all the teachers over to your house for coffee this weekend. See you Saturday." I laughed, and Abby waved goodbye to us, and we waved back.

I helped Zoomer put their shoes and coat on, and we walked hand in hand out of Kid-Land and into a blizzard. My heart was so warm, so full of the love that was poured into my family's cup here every day, that every snowflake in the city could have melted.

TWELVE

Gender Creative Style

The first time I bought a piece of clothing for Zoomer was almost a year before I was even pregnant. Brent and I were in Moab, Utah, with our friends Sean and Raye. We were walking along the sidewalks of Main Street, checking out bookstores and making our way to a restaurant for lunch, when all of a sudden, I screamed. My startled friends and Brent quickly turned to make sure I hadn't been hit by a car, only to find me standing in front of a big glass window, looking in on a shop's display. I turned to look at my travel partners and uttered, "It's the cutest thing I've ever seen."

It was a little white onesie. On it was a campfire, brown logs and red and yellow flames made out of felt. Above the fire, a felt marshmallow on a roasting stick. Like a s'more, the onesie made me feel all warm and toasty inside. I walked away from the storefront and toward the Mexican restaurant we were headed to. I apologized. "Sorry I scared you. But goddamn, that's a cute onesie."

We drank margaritas and ate our lunch and talked about the Jeeping excursion through the red rocks we had gone on that morning. After we finished, we paid our bill and started walking to Sean's Jeep so we could head to the vacation-rental house where we were staying. "I'm going in!" I said as we got close to the little shop with the onesie.

I veered off the sidewalk, walked into the shop, and was greeted by a kind sales associate.

"Hi! I want to buy that campfire-mallow onesie in the window."

They pointed to a small rack and mentioned they had a few different sizes. I walked over, selected a three-to-six-months-size onesie, and put it on the counter to pay.

"I don't even have a kid yet, but this thing is so dang cute, I couldn't resist."

The attendant chuckled. "It is super cute. Your future little one will look adorable in it, I'm sure."

I grabbed my little brown bag with my little white onesie, said "Thanks!" and walked outside with a skip.

A couple of months after our time in Moab, Brent and I were on a road trip along the Pacific Coast Highway in California, on our moon-honey as we called it (a flip of honeymoon, since we did it the week before our wedding instead of after). "We're getting close to Monterey Bay. Want to go to the aquarium?" I asked. Brent said he definitely did, and he followed the signs to get us there.

We explored the aquarium for a couple of hours, and then it was time to get back on the road. As one does, we exited through the gift shop. There was ocean-themed everything. After slowly walking by the sea lion coffee mugs and the jellyfish Christmas tree ornaments, I spotted a section with children's clothing and felt compelled to walk over. Brent and I had started discussing, with seriousness, having a kid. And I was suddenly noticing children's clothing now whenever I was within a half-mile radius of it.

There were onesies and T-shirts and hoodies for infants, toddlers, kids, and teens. I looked at the gradual size increases and felt excited about the possibility of having my own child who would grow through these stages. I saw a green T-shirt with an octopus on it that said "Monterey Bay Aquarium."

As I walked up to it, Brent approached behind me and said, "That's cute."

I took the shirt off the rack. "It is cute. Should we get one for our future kid?"

Brent smiled. "Yeah, let's do it." He looked at the different sizes and grabbed one that was 2T. "I think it would be cutest on a little toddler running around."

I nodded in agreement. "Definitely." We bought the shirt. And when we got home from our road trip, I put it on a shelf in our closet, next to the campfire onesie.

Once I was pregnant and after I had Zoomer, the hand-me-downs started rolling in. My sister gave us a few boxes of clothes that Mara had outgrown. Some friends of ours gave us a couple of big plastic totes of previously loved baby clothes.

I started strolling the children's clothing aisles at stores, walking through all the sections. I knew that I wasn't going to be assigning a gender to my baby, and I wasn't going to be assigning one side of the store either. I'd wander through the areas with clothes marketed to boys and the side marketed to girls, finding onesies and leggings and tops that I thought were cute.

My first priority when shopping for clothing for Zoomer was comfort. I didn't want to put Zoomer in anything that might be stiff or scratchy or too warm or not warm enough. My second priority was finding items that weren't too complicated to get on or off. I tried to avoid buttons, opting for zippers, snaps, and easy-to-get-on options. After comfort and ease were taken care of, that's when I could have fun with baby clothes, choosing bright colors and funky patterns.

Brent introduced me to an Australian brand called BONDS, which makes an incredible article of clothing called the Wondersuit. Wondersuits are truly one-piece wonders, with an easy zip from bottom to top, and *the* coolest patterns and prints I've ever seen for kids' clothes. Bananas, sharks, fluorescent flowers, planets, rainbow stripes, you name it. The company doesn't market to "boys" or "girls" for baby clothes; the onesies are simply for little ones. Once I discovered Wondersuits, Zoomer practically lived in them. They're so soft and cozy and even have little flaps that geniusly convert into mitten- and sock-like covers for babies' hands and feet.

After fumbling around with snaps in the first month of Zoomer's life, skipping a snap and having to start over in the middle of the night, I said to hell with these and pretty much converted to simple shirts, leggings, and Wondersuits. As gender creative parents, we do try to put our money where our mouths are and support brands that aren't promoting gender stereotypes.

In the first two years of Zoomer's life, Brent and I made most of the decisions about their clothing. We bought the clothes that we thought were comfy, practical, and cute. For the most part, no pattern, print, or color was off-limits. Fabric doesn't have a gender. Pink and purple are not just for girls, and blue and black are not just for boys. Sometimes I see a pattern and have a quick flash of "Oh, that's for boys" or "That's for girls," but then I ask myself why I thought that—just because it's on the boys' rack? Or in the girls' section? Since when are lightning bolts for boys or dragonflies for girls? As if lightning or dragonflies need to get caught up in this gender binary mess. Yes—these are absolutely the types of monologues I have in my head at TJ Maxx. Ultimately, if I like it, I buy it.

Brent and I aren't big fans of words on clothes in the first place, but especially with a gender creative babe, we don't buy clothes that have gendered or sexualized phrases on them. I cringe when I see shirts with the words "Flirt" or "Heartbreaker" or "Lock Up Your Daughters" or "Daddy Says No Dating till I'm 40."

I've noticed that the clothes that are marketed to girls might have more fun, colorful prints, but the material is often of lower quality and thinner fabric: narrower shirts and thinner pants and leggings than the thicker, more durable clothing in the section marketed to boys. "Girl" shorts are often much shorter than "boy" shorts. Underwear that is marketed to girls is often paper thin; it's as if it's the training wheels for a life in which women are expected to wear uncomfortable underwear. You're much more likely to find sparkles in the section marketed to girls, and the colors are often pastels, and patterns are often florals or hearts. I would love to see more clothing brands introduce more colors and more unique patterns and prints.

In the section marketed to boys, there's lots of navy blue and black and gray, with some red and yellow thrown in. The prints are often in the dinosaur, robot, or emergency response vehicle realm, which is fine, but I want more. While browsing the racks marketed to toddler-aged boys, I thought, *It's like someone shrank the wardrobe of a bank manager.* Collared button-down shirts, suspenders, and khakis. Kids get one chance to be kids. My vote is high-quality, durable, comfortable clothes that can keep up with them and that come in incredibly fun and colorful prints. There are, of course, some great brands that are creating clothes like this, but we need mainstream big brands to cool it on the "girls' clothes" and the "boys' clothes" and just make more clothes for kids.

Once Zoomer turned two, they started having opinions about what they wanted to wear. If we were shopping in the store, we'd let Zoomer loose and see what they gravitated toward. If we're shopping for shorts, we grab options from all over the store and let Z pick the pairs they like most. Zoomer likes being comfortable and wearing clothes with fun colors and mismatched prints, and they wander through all the aisles, unaware of the arbitrary boundary that has been set up by society. The outfits they choose bring a smile to my face. Zoomer wants a say in everything: their underwear, shirts, bottoms, socks, hats, shoes, hair clips, pajamas, and sunglasses. And we give them that. We enthusiastically support Zoomer in expressing themself however feels best.

For months, their favorite shirt was the green one with "the octa-puth" that their parents bought them before they were born. After they wore it for two days straight, we'd have to bribe them to take it off so we could wash it. Bittersweetly, Zoomer is outgrowing it. Now we're planning a road trip back to the Monterey Bay Aquarium so this stylish child of mine can pick out a shirt in the next size up.

THIRTEEN

Stepping into the Spotlight

I n May 2016, TEDxSaltLakeCity put out a call for speakers for their fifth event. Zoomer wasn't even two months old. I was exhausted and a few weeks away from going back to work full time. I was spending every spare minute completing my dissertation. What I didn't need to do was apply to be a speaker at a TEDx event.

Yet I wanted to be a public advocate for gender creative parenting. I wanted to help people understand the big reasons why we wanted to parent this way—that children deserve the opportunity to define their own identity and that no child should experience disparities because of their gender. I had a supportive network. I studied gender and sexuality and had experience distilling information into accessible lessons as a university instructor. I had thick skin. I knew that this way of parenting was important and that if more people knew about it, if more people felt confident that they could do it, too, they would. I felt a responsibility to put myself out there.

When I told Brent that I wanted to apply to be a speaker and give a talk on gender creative parenting, he looked a little surprised.

"Do you think you have time?" he asked.

"I one hundred percent do not have the time, but I think it could be such a great resource for other parents that I feel like I should at least apply."

Brent was concerned about how thin I was spreading myself. But, ever the supporter, he agreed I should apply. "If you get accepted," Brent compromised, "every new idea you have for the rest of the year needs to be run by me and Raye, and we have to vote on whether or not you can do it before you say yes."

I thought about his request for a moment and nodded in agreement. I knew he was joking, but it was actually a good idea. "Deal."

I submitted my idea, which made it to the next round, where I had to create a ninety-second video. In my submission, a tiny Zoomer is in my arms, my hair is in a ponytail, I have no makeup on, and I'm in clothes that are arguably one step up from pajamas. I am pretty sure we took one take—maybe two. If parenting had taught me anything, it was how to be more efficient and loosen my grip on perfectionism. I can't remember exactly what I said in the video, but it must have had something to do with why I thought gender creative parenting was such a great idea. I uploaded it to my computer and emailed it to the speaker selection committee.

During Memorial Day weekend, Brent, Zoomer, and I headed to Wyoming for our first getaway as a trio. We stayed in a motel in Jackson Hole and explored the Grand Teton and Yellowstone National Parks for a few days. Zoomer was just ten weeks new. I remember quickly checking my email on my phone as we drove along a highway with bison in the fields beneath the majestic Tetons. I saw there was a message in my inbox: "TEDxSaltLakeCity Final Decision."

"Brent, the TEDx speaker decision has been made—should I check this now?"

"Of course!" Brent excitedly encouraged. He was driving, and I was in the back seat with a snoozy Zooms.

I opened the email and saw that I had been selected as a speaker.

"I'm in!" I said to Brent. I was excited but definitely nervous about the work that I would need to put in over the next four months to make it as good as I possibly could.

"That's so exciting, babelove! I'm proud of you."

I felt a wave of fear. I had an infant; I had just started a full-time job; I didn't have predictable childcare; I was conducting my dissertation research; and now I had to write a script, memorize it, perform it for nineteen hundred people live, and have it uploaded to YouTube to live on the internet forever. It was a recipe for disaster.

I wanted to do it, but more importantly, I felt like I had to do it. I wished there had been a TEDx talk for me to share with my family and friends about gender creative parenting when Brent and I first decided to go for it. An opportunity to create the resource that I'd desperately wanted had presented itself, so come hell or high water, I was going to do it.

I wrote a dozen versions of the script. I had debates with my speaker mentor, a neuroscientist, about what's innate and what's socialized and how sometimes it's hard to tell. I incorporated some of his feedback, and I flushed some of it down the toilet. After multiple revisions, I was getting close.

My friends Derek and Raye came over and helped me workshop the script for an entire day. After two months, I felt confident that I had the script where I wanted it, and then I had to memorize it. No notes were allowed on the TEDx stage. I had never had to do anything like it. The last thing I had memorized every word of were the lyrics of "Out Tonight" after I saw *Rent* in 2005, and at least that had a repeating chorus!

I storyboarded the talk. I made flash cards. I read the script when I woke up and recited it every time I was in the shower. I recorded myself reading the script, and on the train to work, I would put headphones on and listen to the recording, trying to keep up and remember the next word, the next line. For an entire month, instead of bedtime stories, my darling five-month-old Zoomer sat in their crib, watching their mom act out a story. A story I wanted the whole world to hear. A story I was telling to make Zoomer's life better. A story I hoped would make a lot of kids' lives better.

My fellow TEDxSaltLakeCity speakers became my dear friends that summer. We gladly listened to each other's talks over and over and over again in the practice auditorium and in the parking lot at dusk. We suggested word changes and body language; we brought each other to tears, some caused by laughter and others by pain. I got to watch Lance Allred's talk, "What Is Your Polygamy?"[20] and Piper Christian's "Tell a Story, Protect the Planet"[21] come to life.

On a Saturday in September, I walked onto the stage at Kingsbury Hall and delivered my message in the form of a talk titled "Want Gender Equality? Let's Get Creative."[22] My parents and siblings were in the audience. Brent was in the audience. My friends were in the audience. And a whole lot of people I didn't know were in the audience. They listened; they chuckled; they nodded; they applauded.

When I finished, I walked off the stage and was met by my speaker mentor, who was smiling and opened his arms to hug me. "You did great," he said.

Afterward, people approached me to tell me how my talk made them feel. A pediatrician told me he wished more parents could hear my message, that if parents cared as much about limiting gender stereotypes as they cared about reducing screen time and sugar intake, we could achieve equality a lot quicker. "I couldn't agree more," I told him. He asked if he could give me a hug, and I gladly accepted.

Liv brought Zoomer to the event during the lunch break, and an elderly person approached us and said, "Zoomer, I was skeptical when your mom first started talking, but by the end, I realized you are a very lucky kid."

I was nervous about the video being uploaded online. The crowd at the TEDx event had been friendly, which was to be expected. Now my story was going to be out there for anyone. A couple of months after the live talk, the video was posted online. The view count clicked up by one thousand to two thousand viewers a month. The wave of hate that I was bracing for didn't come. Or, rather, I didn't go looking for it because I never read the YouTube comments. "Never read the comments" was a mantra I was committed to. Very few people went out of their way to find my email address and let me know, usually in one sentence filled with typos, that I was the worst. Instead of responding, I deleted the cruel messages. Another wave enveloped me, one of love and gratitude.

I connected with people who found my talk and were able to use it as a resource in talking with their families about their plans to do gender creative parenting. I heard from professors who were using the video in their classrooms. I heard from therapists who thanked me for creating a resource to share with parents of trans and nonbinary youth. I heard from nonbinary and trans adults who said they wished they had been raised like Zoomer. I heard from parents who said they were treating their children more equitably. I had created something that people found helpful and inspiring, and I was proud. Tired, but proud.

~

Zoomer was six months old, and Brent and I were hyperaware of how rampant gender stereotypes were in advertising, especially gender stereotypes in childhood and parenting. One day, Brent came home from the grocery store, and as he unloaded the groceries from the bag and put things in the fridge and cupboards, he began to complain.

"When a company has a slogan like 'Choosy Moms Choose Jif' or that something is 'Mom Approved,' it makes me feel like I'm a second-rate parent because I'm a dad. I hate all these ads and commercials that make dads out to be incompetent and hopeless at caring for their children. It's bullshit."

I frowned. "I know. I'm sorry. It sucks. Hopefully you bought a different brand of peanut butter?"

Brent smirked. "You're damn right I did!"

We had been paying attention to how products were marketed and opted for the ones that weren't trying to capitalize on stereotypes. We gravitated toward brands that didn't target moms, but rather parents or caretakers in general. We gave our money to companies that sent inclusive messages, that were trying to challenge stereotypes, not perpetuate them.

Brent and I went on to do a presentation on the topic of gender in design and marketing for a Design Week event, where all types of creatives come together from different design disciplines, like fashion, graphic and digital, architecture, interior, and advertising, to be inspired and collaborate. We wanted to help Salt Lake creatives think more critically about the role they can play in designing more inclusive products and ads and culture.

Brent hates public speaking. Hates it. He doesn't like being the center of attention in any way. If he could skip his birthday, he probably would. Brent is fully supportive of anything I want to do as an advocate for gender creative parenting, but he made it very clear to me: "You are the spokesperson, Kyl. Not me." He reads everything I write and has helpful discussions with me prior to interviews, but he would rather do *anything* than have a microphone in front of his face. But Brent is an incredibly talented designer, and I wanted his expertise and partnership to make this event as effective as possible, and he got on board.

On a weeknight in October, while Zoom was at home with Liv, Brent, who tabled his disdain for public speaking, stood next to me in front of a crowd of designers, marketing and advertising professionals, and students as we talked about the differences between sex and gender. We described the gender spectrum and challenged the gender binary. We discussed the history of gender roles and stereotypes as they relate to consumerism. We asked the crowd to question their assumptions, consider their actual target audience, and ask themselves who is missing and how they can make their designs more accessible. We encouraged a room full of creatives to design the future of gender equality and inclusion.

We met some incredible creatives that night who vowed to go to work the next day and do better. They wanted to make sure the imagery on their websites was diverse—opting to use the photo of the young female doctor of color instead of the overused older White man. They wanted to make sure their drop-down boxes reflected the reality of their customers, doing away with the binary male or female options and adding categories like nonbinary, genderqueer, and intersex and space for people to input their identity if they didn't feel represented by the options presented. We challenged them to consider if asking about sex or gender was necessary at all.

Two and a half years after that event, I got an email. It was from a designer named Joshua, who was writing to tell me that they were working on a project to redesign the maps at a large health center that would help patients and visitors find their way around. Joshua wrote,

> I remembered that years ago I attended your presentation Designing Gender: The Art of Equality. We've been using antiquated restroom symbols—the ones depicting a "man" and "woman." I'm scouring the internet and can't seem to find a standard, gender inclusive restroom symbol. I may end up having to make up my own, but if you had any suggestions I would love to hear them.
>
> P.S. At the very least, I wanted to share how you've helped a designer out there in your local community be sensitive to these kinds of things.

I wrote Joshua back and thanked them for taking the steps to be inclusive in their work. I suggested using a toilet icon—it's universally recognized, gender free, and gets the job done. I said I'd love to see the finished product and would be happy to brainstorm if they felt stuck. When I pressed "Send" on the email, I smiled. I felt grateful that I was a part of this designer's story, and years later they were incorporating our message into their projects, and this health center would be a safer, more inclusive space for the patients it served.

I'm a fan of the "If you see something, say something" motto, but in both ways. If I see something that is exclusionary, I'll send a polite message to a manager and make a recommendation for something more inclusive. On the other side of that, though, if I see a company doing a great job, using inclusive imagery and terminology, I send a thank-you note, just a few words to say that I noticed and appreciated it. Consumers have the power to suggest small changes that can lead to big ones.

Stepping into the spotlight as a public advocate for gender creative parenting was terrifying. But I had such conviction that gender creative parenting could contribute to changing the world for the better that I knew I had to spread the message as often and as far as I could. Being a part of this movement—being a part of creating a more inclusive world that celebrates diversity and relentlessly fights for equality—would be my greatest achievement.

FOURTEEN

Creating Spaces

As we got into our parenting routine, Brent and I noticed that many kids' playgroups were advertised in a way that assumed it would be a mom bringing the child(ren). Things like Mom and Me Yoga and Mommy and Baby Story Time perpetuate the assumption that women are the ones most involved in staying home with kids or coordinating their extracurricular activities, playdates, and attendance at events. I'd frown when I'd see these posters in the library or on a community bulletin board. What about the dads? The grandparents? The Moddies and Zazas and other nonbinary parents of the world? In my experience, as someone who equally shares parenting with my partner, I didn't have a need for a "mom group"; what I'm all for is gender-expansive spaces for caregivers and their little ones.

I wanted a space where families could gather and know there was a conscious effort being made not to stereotype children, not to assume caregivers are straight or cisgender or partnered or monogamous, and to create a space to build some sense of community. We had our first gender creative playgroup when Zoomer was about six months old. We made an announcement on Instagram and created a Facebook event. We shared it with our friends and reached out to the LGBTQ Resource

Center at the University of Utah, the Pride Center in Salt Lake City, and anyone else I could think of who might be interested in sharing the event.

We hosted the playgroup at Liberty Park, a huge public space in Salt Lake City. We told people to look for the purple and silver balloons, which we tied to a picnic table. We brought some water and snacks, laid blankets down on the grass, and placed toys and books on them. Some of my friends from work showed up with their kids and another friend who was trying to get pregnant. One of our friends brought his two small daughters; the older one, a preschooler, was wearing a Princess Anna dress from *Frozen*.

In a somewhat embarrassed tone, he said, "Of course my daughter wants to wear a princess dress at a gender creative playgroup."

I reassured him. "It's great she's wearing the Anna dress. It's what she wants to wear, and you're supporting her in that; that's the point of this, just letting kids be themselves."

He sat his younger daughter down on the blanket next to Zoomer. They were about the same age and played together, passing leaves that had fallen from the trees to each other and sharing Cheerios. We all caught up, talking about the milestones our children were reaching—what funky crawling techniques they each had, what hilarious things they said. We asked each other about work and upcoming plans. It was a typical playgroup, but one that had a soft glow of inclusivity all around it.

We host a playgroup every few months. There are always new families: some we know through work or Z's school, some who we've met online or who have been told about us through another community organization. While there are usually kids who have been assigned a gender or who identify as boys or girls, there are also kids who are non-binary, exploring the possibilities of gender, or socially transitioning. In the first year, there weren't any other gender creative parents attending the playgroups, but by the second year, I had met two other Utah-based gender creative families.

One of my favorite playgroups was in November 2018. Zoomer was two and a half years old, and we got to meet four other gender creative families in person—friends we had made online. My friends Bobby and Lesley flew to Salt Lake from Brooklyn, New York, with their baby, Sojourner Wildfire. My friend Ari flew to Salt Lake from Orlando, Florida, with their baby, Sparrow, and their nine-year-old, Hazel. I had met Bobby, Lesley, and Ari through the Facebook group for parents raising their children with they/them pronouns, and they had flown to Salt Lake so we could present on a panel about gender creative parenting at the genderevolution conference.

Our families played together all weekend. We attended the conference together on Saturday, presented about gender creative parenting, and shared our stories to a room full of interested and supportive people, eager for an alternative to the mainstream way of binary-gendered parenting that didn't resonate with them.

On Sunday, our three families hosted a gender creative playgroup at the International Peace Gardens in Salt Lake City. A local gender creative family showed up, and another family drove two hours to attend. My good friend Lance, a retired NBA player whom I'd met through TEDx, brought his son to play. There were six gender creative children, three nonbinary parents who used they/them pronouns, and eight cisgender parents and kids. We all played on the playground, drank hot chocolate, ate vegan doughnuts, and strolled through the International Peace Gardens looking at the sculptures and playing in the piles of leaves. Everyone's pronouns were respected, and everyone's gender identity and expression were celebrated. It was a beautiful morning dedicated to making new friends and just letting parents be parents and kids be kids. That's my kind of playgroup.

~

A few months before Zoomer turned two, we were invited to their friend Arthur's third birthday party at Tiny Tumblers, a children's gym in Salt Lake. We had never been to Tiny Tumblers before; we walked in on that Saturday afternoon, and Zoomer discovered their new favorite place. They were swinging on bars and walking across balance beams; they were running on mats and chasing and popping bubbles. They absolutely *loved* it.

After ninety minutes of birthday fun, we went home, and Zoomer would not stop asking about it. "I want to go to Tiny Tumblers" would be the first thing they'd say when they woke up and the last thing they'd say before they fell asleep. Weeks after the birthday party, I was driving on a road near Tiny Tumblers. Zoomer piped up from the back seat, having recognized where we were, and excitedly asked, "We going to Tiny Tumblers?" I was shocked that Zoomer understood where we were. Z was sending a clear message that they wanted to spend more time at the gym, so we decided we should have their upcoming birthday party there and make this kid's dreams come true.

I visited the Tiny Tumblers' website and saw that I could book a birthday party online. I clicked on the button and started filling out the form. It asked for Zoomer's name and their age, and then it asked for their gender and gave "Male" and "Female" options. I left it blank and clicked "Next," but it wouldn't let me proceed to the next page without selecting a binary sex. Hmph.

I have a rule for myself regarding these drop-down boxes, a few things I consider before I will select a sex or gender marker for Zoomer. I ask myself, *Is it totally necessary for this organization to know Zoomer's sex? Can I get around this?* And *If they were to know Zoomer's sex, might it influence how they treat them?*

Zoomer wouldn't be using their reproductive organs on the uneven bars or balance beam, so Tiny Tumblers didn't need to know their sex.

And Zoomer hadn't told me their gender identity yet, so I couldn't help the gym out there. I looked for the phone number of the gym on the site, tapped it into my cell phone, and called them.

A friendly person answered, introduced themself as Phoebe, and asked how they could help.

"Hi, Phoebe. I was just online trying to book a birthday party for my kid, and when I tried to leave the gender question blank, it wouldn't let me proceed. We didn't assign a gender to our kid, and they haven't told us their gender yet, so I just thought I'd call and see if there's any way I can book this party without having to select a gender."

Phoebe was quick. I was impressed. "Oh, I'm so sorry! I hate that that question is on the form. It's a corporate thing. Of course you don't have to choose a gender. Let me get you in our system! What is your little one's name?"

"Their name is Zoomer."

"Great. And what day did you want to have their party?"

Impressive. Phoebe had picked up on my use of gender-neutral pronouns and didn't skip a beat.

"March 24 if it's available."

"We've got a three p.m. party spot available. What two colors would you like for the decorations—things like tablecloths, plates and cups, and stuff?"

"Oh, one second. I'll ask Zoomer." Zoomer was playing on the living room floor in front of me. "Zoomer, honey, what's your favorite color today?" Zoomer looked up at me from their little plastic picnic basket and said, "Pink!"

"Great. What other color?" I asked.

"Ortja," they said enthusiastically, holding up a little plastic orange slice.

"We'll go with pink and orange, please," I told Phoebe.

"How old will Zoomer be?" Phoebe asked.

"They'll be two!" I responded, partly in disbelief of how quickly time was flying.

O ver the next few weeks, we gave invitations to all the kids in Zoomer's class at school and invited our family and friends with kids. My family drove the four hours from Saint George to celebrate Zoomer's upcoming next trip around the sun. I remember feeling really warm and squishy when my stepmom, April, texted, **What does my little grandbaby want for their birthday?** There's something about seeing gender-neutral pronouns typed out or written that proves that my family is conscious of actively supporting us.

Zoomer woke up from their nap, and Brent got them in a little fluorescent flower-print Wondersuit. We told Zoomer, "Guess what? It's time for your birthday party at Tiny Tumblers!" Zoomer's sleepy eyes turned alert, and they jumped up and down and clapped their hands. They were pumped.

Twenty kids and their families piled into Tiny Tumblers. Everyone kicked off their shoes, and the teachers miraculously got all the toddlers to sit in a circle on the mat. Phoebe asked each kid to introduce themself and add an ingredient to a big imaginary birthday cake batter for Zoomer. It went something like this: "I Oona . . . blueberries!" Then everyone would pretend to throw blueberries into the center of the circle and pat the ground a few times.

"I Galen . . . chocolate!" Pat, pat, pat.

"Savannah . . . Spider-Man!" Pat, pat, pat.

"I Zoomie . . . abocado!" Pat, pat, pat.

"Daniel . . . fruit snacks."

"River . . . quesadilla!"

And on and on it went until we had the most disgusting imaginary cake batter that there's ever been.

The kids ran around the gym, laughing maniacally. They joined in on a few organized activities with songs and a rainbow parachute game.

There were remarkably few collisions and tears. All the parents chatted while the youngsters expended a million kilowatts of energy.

"It's time for cake and ice cream!" Phoebe got everyone's attention, and all the little ones and their parents filed into the party room. There were tiny tables and chairs set out with pink and orange tablecloths and pink and orange paper cups and plates. My best friend, Raye, had called us on FaceTime two weeks earlier and asked Zoomer what kind of cake they wanted.

"Choo-choo cake," Z answered without skipping a beat.

Raye confirmed. "OK, Zoomer Coyote, you want a train cake?"

Zoomer nodded on FaceTime. "Ya! Choo-choo train cake!"

Raye smiled. "I'm gonna get you a train cake, baby!"

In true Raye fashion, she had a two-tiered custom cake made for Zoomer. We put a big number-2-shaped candle on top of the cake and lit it, and Phoebe turned out the light. I held the heavy masterpiece of a cake and started walking toward Zoomer, singing, "Happy birthday to you," and the whole room started singing along. I set the cake down in front of Zoomer, and we encouraged them to blow out the candle. They hadn't quite worked out how to blow, and it ended up being more of a wet, horse-like *bpbpbpbppbp*, so Brent helped blow the candle out, and everyone clapped.

As everyone ate cake and ice cream, I looked around the room, and time slowed down. When I was pregnant, I hadn't had the foresight to imagine what my child's second birthday party would look like. But here I stood, two years into parenting—gender creative parenting—and we were surrounded by a group of people who loved us and supported us. Zoomer sat at the table, laughing with their friends as they stole bites of cake from each other's plates. Zoomer was adored. My dad walked across the room and gave me a hug. He looked me in the eyes and said, "I love my little grandbaby so much. Look at them. You've done so good. I'm proud of you." We stood and looked over at Zoomer Coyote, an incredible little two-year-old who had completely rocked our world.

FIFTEEN

The Media Hoopla

The first media request came while I was on family leave after Zoomer was born. A former work colleague of mine was now a host on a morning show in Texas. She emailed me, saying she pitched the idea of a story about gender creative parenting to her producers, and they all loved it. She had seen Zoomer's birth announcement on Instagram. She asked if I would be willing to be interviewed for a segment. I was still learning what my child's different cries meant, so the idea of a news interview felt a little overwhelming and premature.

Later that day, I brought it up to Brent when he got home from work. I told him I was not interested in doing a news show right now. I'd rather just say what I have to say on the blog and Instagram. "I also don't want to be on millions of Texans' televisions, like, 'Hi, I became a parent four hours ago, let me tell you how I have all the answers,'" I said, making Brent laugh.

"I am not ready for the news yet either," Brent said. "I'll support you when you're ready, but I think we have to be really careful because not everyone who will want to interview you has our best interest in mind."

I nodded. "Agreed. It's just so weird. We're just trying to protect our kid from stereotypes . . . trying to give our kid the opportunity to explore gender. Is that newsworthy?" I shivered at the thought of being in a news studio, being counted down—three, two, one—to when I'd be on live, with an interviewer who had no interest in gender creative parenting but a big interest in making me out to be a spectacle.

I didn't want to be clickbait for a media outlet, an outrageous headline that wasn't representative of our actual experience. I had control over my story through my own words on the blog and Instagram. I wasn't interested in doing an interview that would get sliced and diced into a reedited clip. I wasn't going to let a morning news anchor who didn't know me have the pleasure of saying, "Look at these wackadoodle parents!"

For the first two years of Zoomer's life, I turned down all media requests. About a dozen magazine writers and producers from radio and television stations reached out to me through Instagram or email, asking if I would do an interview. I preferred to have control over our story. I could choose the personal moments of our life that I wanted to share with a public audience. I could craft the message I wanted to send through accessible, positive, bite-size servings of gender creative parenting in the captions and stories of our Instagram account. I liked being the one in charge of our family's narrative and reach, but I understood that at some point, I would probably have to surrender control if I wanted to contribute to gender creative parenting becoming more mainstream.

On February 20, 2018, one month before Zoomer's second birthday, I got an email from a journalist, Alex Morris, asking if I would do an interview. My friend Bobby, a fellow gender-open parent, had been talking with Alex for a feature in *New York* magazine about this parenting philosophy, this movement of giving children the opportunity to come to their own gender identity and expression. Bobby had shared my TEDx talk with Alex and told her he had used it to educate his own family members and friends when he was introducing them to his parenting plans.

Alex had watched the talk and wanted to interview me, not only as someone doing gender creative parenting but also as someone with a PhD in sociology, whose job is to study gender within social systems. Bobby asked me to be another voice in the feature. He said he felt good about Alex, whom he'd met through a mutual friend. He reassured me that she was supportive of what we were doing and would tell our stories in a respectful way.

I talked to Brent about it. I told him I might be ready to do an interview, and I wanted to support Bobby. Brent deferred the decision to me and said he was OK with me doing the interview if I decided I wanted to. I looked up other stories Alex had written—one about Halsey, one about Evan Rachel Wood. Alex wrote about gender and sexuality and abortion in a way that cued to me that she and I were on the same wavelength about a lot of things, so I responded to her request and agreed to talk.

With Alex in New York and me in Utah, we had our first conversation through a video chat that lasted for nearly three hours. I know journalists are supposed to be friendly and get you to feel comfortable opening up so they can get the juicy, vulnerable parts of your story. Alex was good at her job. I genuinely enjoyed talking with her.

There were emails, texts, and calls afterward for sending additional resources and fact-checking. I laughed out loud when Isla, a *New York* magazine fact-checker, called me to confirm that, yes, Zoomer's stuffed horse was, in fact, named Nay Nay Douglas the Airport Horse, and we used they/them pronouns for Nay Nay.

Before hanging up the phone, Isla told me that they had taken gender studies courses in college, and they were very excited to see this story being told; it was inspiring to them as a young person to have role models showing alternative ways of parenting outside the traditional binary.

I thanked Isla for saying that and assured them, "Gender creative parenting is the best parenting decision I've made. If you do become a parent and want to parent this way, you'll be in great company." I had a feeling that this feature was going to help inspire other young people, other future parents who wanted something different.

Another *New York* magazine staffer, a photo editor named Matt, emailed me. Matt wanted a photo for the feature and had selected a few photos from our Instagram account that they thought would work well. It was uncomfortable, trying to choose a photo of our family that hundreds of thousands of people would see, either in the glossy pages of the issue or on the digital pages of The Cut, a website operated by *New York* magazine. One thing I was certain of was I didn't want Zoomer alone in the photo. I told Matt that I wanted to make sure the photo was of us as a family. Matt was respectful of our request, and we all agreed on one photo—a picture of our little trio in Cottonwood Canyon.

Alex told me the feature would be out soon and would be online through The Cut a day or two after the magazine hit the stands. I woke up early the day it came out, and I downloaded a digital version of the entire issue so I could read the feature for the first time; it would take another two weeks before the issue arrived at the Barnes and Noble in Salt Lake City, where Brent and I would buy three copies.

It was bizarre seeing a photo of us and reading our story in a magazine that I had loved for years.[23] I felt good about how it turned out. I felt like Alex honored our story and that we were well represented. I was one of a handful of parents who gave an interview for the piece. My friends Bobby, Leah, and Andrea all talked about their motivations and shared anecdotes. Our stories wove in and out of each other's; all our parenting decisions headed toward a common goal of supporting our children in finding their own way to their gender. I sat on the couch with a cup of coffee and read it again.

The "It's a Theyby!" article was released online, and the response from The Cut readers was generally positive. I was open to doing the interview for *New York* magazine because it's a progressive publication for a progressive audience. The positive reception was a self-fulfilling prophecy. My dad sent me a text that said, Read NY Magazine article. Proud of you baby girl. XO. My eyes teared up. I could be a public advocate for gender creative parenting because I had such an incredibly supportive network of family and friends making it easy to do.

At the time the article came out on The Cut, our Instagram, @raisingzoomer, had about a thousand followers. Half of them were our friends, family, colleagues, or former students of mine, and the other half were fellow gender creative parents and progressive and kind online friends we had made all over the world. During that first week of April, our Instagram following ticked up by about five hundred mostly nice folks. I figured that was it. *OK, we told our story. It's out there; some people read it, and a few of them have popped on over to Instagram to follow our journey.* I could now get back to my life. I was naive, to say the least, in my knowledge of how online news happens these days.

Within days of the theyby article being published on The Cut, the story took on a life of its own. Photos of Zoomer were on major news sources in dozens of countries with headlines like "Parents Keep Baby's Gender Secret from Even Their Own Family," "What's in This Kid's Nappy?" and "Hipster Parents Co-opting Queer Parenting Practices." Some spin-off stories took quotes out of context, spelled my name wrong, and removed my credentials. I was made out to be an attention-seeking, money-hungry mom, accused of abusing my child and setting Zoomer up for irreversible psychological damage.

I wouldn't consider my parenting practice "news," but in the day and age of twenty-four-hour online media content, news sources are looking for anything click worthy. Over the course of a few weeks, I watched as our story and photos of my family spread all across the globe. We were in Italian news and Portuguese news, German, French, and Brazilian news. Brent was tracking the story, looking for where it would pop up next. I was trying to ignore what was happening. Out of all the families in the feature, it was us—Brent, Zoomer, and me—who went viral.

I didn't see it coming. I didn't realize how unethical media outlets had become. I had no idea that someone could pluck a photo from my Instagram and publish it in a newspaper with "quotes" from me taken from the article on The Cut, my blog, or my Instagram captions but disguised as if I had given the media outlet an interview.

I should have known better. Doing *one* interview was the green light for anyone to make news of my family. More than a year after The Cut published the article, I still get alerts about new stories being published about us. I don't regret doing the *New York* magazine interview; I just wish I had been more prepared for what would happen next.

It's a bizarre feeling going from having a fairly anonymous life to one where, overnight, millions of people have an opinion about you as a person and as a parent, based on a speck of information. Brent and I made a pact not to talk about the media shitshow around Zoomer. When Zoomer was awake, we played with them, snuggled them, and put on a brave face. Our sweet little two-year-old was completely unaware of what their parents were dealing with. Brent would hug me in the kitchen and tell me that I was an incredible parent. I'd let him know he was too. And then we'd climb into bed every night with a new load of strangers' criticism to process.

One journalist with the HuffPost UK was thoughtful and ethical enough to send me a few questions and say, "I'm not going to publish anything about you without your permission." She gave me the opportunity to clear up a few misconceptions about my parenting that I was watching rip through the news. I was able to answer her questions through email and squash some superficial assumptions, like that we don't allow our child to wear pink or blue. That article was posted on April 10, about a week after the media gates had swung open. The activity around our Instagram account came in waves; the strength and temperature of the wave varied, depending on how the article was written and who the audience was. The HuffPost UK wave wasn't enormous, and fortunately it was predominately positive (because I essentially wrote the damn article).[24]

Two weeks after the original article was posted, I woke up, checked my phone, and saw a message from Rachel, a friend of ours in Australia. She said she just heard us being talked about on her favorite Australian podcast and read an article about gender creative parenting on its website. I panicked. I knew that the news would shatter Brent. Our family being thrust into the spotlight was taking a toll on him, and he wasn't ready for us to be news in his home country.

I wasn't about to wake Brent up to tell him. I'd wait until after he had coffee in his system.

He seemed to be in a moderately good mood when he woke up, considering we had stayed awake, teaching cyberbullies about the differences between sex and gender in our Instagram comment section, until well past midnight. Brent suggested we go have breakfast at Publik Kitchen. We threw some clothes on, and the three of us got in the car and headed to the restaurant. We got settled at our table and ordered coffees and breakfast.

I opened with "I need to tell you something."

Brent was getting Zoomer situated with some crayons and a coloring book. He looked at me with a side eye. "What happened?" he asked, now giving me his full attention.

"Well, our story is in Australia now. Rachel sent me a link to a podcast and article from yesterday."

"What podcast? What news source?" He was not happy.

"Oh, nothing major, I don't think. It was posted on something called *MamaMia*."

"*MamaMia*! Kyl! *MamaMia* is major! It's one of the most popular sites in Australia!" He was angry and frustrated. All he wanted was for it to stop, but it just kept going and going, and he was emotionally drained. We both were.

The barista set our coffees down. Brent, who is typically the politest human in the world and thanks people three times for each act, was so distracted that he didn't even notice the latte sitting in front of him. His breathing got louder, and his idiosyncrasies signaled to me that his veins were being filled with anxiety.

He asked, "When did you find out? Why are you just telling me now? Why are you telling me here? I'm hungry!"

"I'm sorry. I didn't know you would be this upset. Do you want to go outside and get some air?" I offered.

Our life sucked at the moment. We couldn't catch a breath. We were exposed in the international spotlight. Every new article felt like a stranger opening up our front door and inviting thousands of other strangers into our home each day. Our life was being lurked on and inspected by new people every hour. Many were supportive, many were not, and it was impossible to tell which camp everyone belonged to.

Brent got up from the table and said he'd be back. He walked out the front door of Publik and down the sidewalk for a lap around the block. After several minutes he came back in and sat down.

"I called my mum and told her that she will probably be seeing us in the news." Brent was deflated. "She actually already knew. Kimberley told her. Mum says she's sorry we're dealing with this and to let you know they love us. I should have told her. I think I was hoping that I wouldn't have to because people would stop writing about us, and it wouldn't get to Australia."

I sighed. "Well, it's in Australia; that's for sure. I've turned down two requests to be interviewed on Aussie news today. I'm glad your parents know, but I'm sad they are probably going to see us being made fun of on TV tomorrow morning."

Neither of us wanted this, and we were trying to figure out how to navigate it. Breakfast arrived, and we ate our toast and eggs in silence. The only noise coming from our table was Zoomer's singsongy voice, playing with stickers and a little toy school bus between bites of oatmeal, blissfully ignorant of the exhausting emotional labor their parents were suffering through.

The next day, we woke to thousands of new followers and hundreds of new comments, and the majority of them were awful. This was by far the biggest wave of new activity on our Instagram and the most negative.

Brent did a quick search on his laptop. "Oh shiiiit." He showed me what he was looking at. The headline "Why This Mum and Dad Won't Tell Anyone if Their 'Theyby' Toddler Is a Girl or a Boy" was in huge letters across the screen. Brent looked at me and said, "We're in British tabloids."

The *Daily Mirror*, the *Sun*, and other UK news had picked the story up. I had lived in England for seven months when I was nineteen years old and had worked as a bartender at a pub in a London suburb. I remember my customers would read the *Sun* and the *Daily Mirror* as they gulped pints of beer. The tabloid newspapers have a combined circulation of two million readers a day. The pages are full of lowbrow gossip, opinions, and hyperbolic stories about the royal family and British sports stars and celebrities. I remember feeling sorry for the people whose stories were published in those pages, who became the topic of conversation among millions of British people in kitchens, offices, trains, salons, and pubs across the nation. Never in a thousand years did I imagine I would be the gossip.

That afternoon, while Zoomer napped, Brent and I had a conversation about what we should do about our Instagram account. We entertained the idea of making the account private or even deleting the account. Within two weeks, our following had jumped from one thousand to twelve thousand followers. There had been a flood of support, but the audience-water also looked murkier, knowing there were also hundreds, if not thousands of people who were following us like we were a freak show. We knew there were people lurking in the virtual rafters just wanting to watch how this experiment was going to play out, hoping for a disaster.

We were visible now in a way we hadn't been the month before. Hundreds of people sent us messages, letting us know that they were so grateful to hear about us and gender creative parenting. They wanted an alternative to traditional childhood gender socialization, and we were providing them with a vocabulary and a support network and serving as role models. Nonbinary and transgender folks reached out, telling us they wish they could have been raised the way Zoomer is being raised and encouraged us to stay strong and visible for those who need us. Brent and I decided we needed to keep our account public. Gender creative parenting was becoming a mainstream concept across the globe. How our story spread wasn't ideal, but our story was out there now, and we weren't going anywhere.

That night, Brent gave Zoomer a bath as I cleaned up the kitchen after dinner. We put Z to bed and opened a bottle of wine. After a full day of ignoring the Instagram account and the latest army of English cyberbullies, we decided we were going in. I poured us each a glass of wine, and we sat on our bed with our phones. Brent logged in to his personal Instagram account, and I logged in to @raisingzoomer.

I gave Brent a playful pep talk, like a coach trying to come up with a strategy for winning a match. "OK . . . remember there are a lot of people reading these comments who are interested in doing gender creative parenting. We need to appear like this isn't shaking us to help keep them confident. And there are trans kids in need of a goddamn ally. Any of our responses could be used as a quote in tomorrow's news, so be smart in there!"

Brent took a sip of red wine, smiled with burgundy-stained lips, and said, "You got it! I'll take the comment section under the photo of us three in Cottonwood Canyon. You take the one of Z with the ice cream cone."

I nodded, took a gulp of wine, and started responding to as many comments as I possibly could until my eyelids got so heavy I had to put the phone down and get ready for bed. It was important to me to fight back. I was not about to allow a wave of trolls to destroy the beautiful community I had created. I thought of everyone who needed me to challenge the bullies, to right the wrongs, to fact-check the ignorance—and to somehow attempt to do it all through a loving filter.

Some people felt I was censoring their "free speech" if I deleted their comment or blocked their buddy. What some people call free speech, I call harassment. Someone has the right to say whatever they want about me—sure, go ahead and talk about how I deserve to be institutionalized—but they need to do it on their own platform, not mine.

A handful of reporters and producers reached out every day. Would I do *Good Morning Britain*? Could I do *Fox and Friends*? Would I fly to Washington, DC? Radio in New Zealand? Did I want a documentary made about us? Nope. I was not interested in doing television interviews. It was taking every ounce of energy I had to just get through a day as it was. I wrote the producers and journalists back with the same message: "Thanks for reaching out, but we aren't interested."

Some came back with offers of money: Would I do five minutes for $1,000? $3,000? "No, thanks." I didn't want to add fuel to the fire. I was already seeing how we were being talked about on the news. If someone was genuinely interested in gender creative parenting, they'd find our Instagram and blog and get to know us the way I have presented our story, not the way a ninety-second clip presents us between the weather and information about a car accident causing traffic for commuters.

For months, the story rolled all across the planet, getting picked up by so many outlets, there was no point trying to count. We were news in dozens of different languages on probably every continent except Antarctica, although maybe a South Pole scientist got involved in a Reddit thread about us. I don't know. It was like watching a game of telephone unfold. The further our story got away from the source, the more riddled with inaccuracies it became. At one point, Brent was allegedly a gender studies professor, and I was his student. We had a good laugh about that.

One day at work, my colleague Rebecca came into my office and told me that her partner, Igor, was reading online news from his hometown in Russia that morning. He paused, turning his laptop screen to face Rebecca, and said, "Why is a picture of Kyl in Russian news?"

Later that day, Brent called me and told me about another Russian article. "There's a photo of you in the hospital bed the day Zoomer was born." I simultaneously felt sick to my stomach and like laughing hysterically. How could this be happening? I was shutting down, wishing I could just hide my family for three to six months and emerge after it was all over, yet knowing how important it was for us to stay visible, stay strong, appear unfazed. I was not prepared to have my photos plastered all over the internet for strangers to see and discuss in online news comment sections and around coffeepots at work. I tried to make light of the situations that were starting to become so heavy that I didn't know how much longer I had until I broke.

"What do you think Vladimir Putin thinks about gender creative parenting?" I asked Brent as I sat at my desk, trying to smile through the overwhelmed tears rolling down my face.

I was trying to be an engaged parent and a present partner, work a demanding full-time job, and hold on to the life I'd had a few weeks earlier while this bizarre experience felt like a tidal wave hovering over me. Friends, former college classmates, and acquaintances I hadn't heard from in years kept forwarding me articles and podcasts that they came across, screenshots of heated Facebook debates with me as the topic of conversation. My typical resilience was having trouble keeping up with the situation. With every day that passed and with each new wave of attention, Brent's anxiety increased as my confidence took blow after blow.

I spent hours every morning before Zoomer woke up and every night after putting Z to bed responding to comments and attempting to inject some correct information into the threads on Instagram, where so many strangers felt emboldened to attack me. I refused to look at comments on the actual publications' websites; I had control over our Instagram, and that was all I had the time for.

People were reaching out to me, saying they wanted to practice gender creative parenting. The next comment would be about how my kid should be taken from me. I was committed to staying kind and unrattled in the comment section. I knew that there were people watching me, and how I handled the situation could make or break someone's decision to think parenting this way was a good idea. I just reminded myself that what I was doing was what I knew to be best for my family and that people who didn't agree would get over it.

Interestingly, there were several people who initially came to our account writing mean comments and attacking our supporters. They were brutal. But then Brent and I would engage with them and encourage them to read more about the differences and nuances of sex and gender and to consider how gender stereotypes were affecting them and their own kids, and we would answer their questions without escalating the situation or calling them names like they called us.

On several occasions, these people who started out loathing us apologized to us, saying they hadn't understood and had decided to lash out instead of opening themselves up to learning. They returned and went to bat for us in the comments, telling other mean commenters, "I thought Kyl and Brent were nuts, too, but now I get it, and I think they are doing an amazing thing for Zoomer." It was wild to witness.

After the media hoopla, my fear ticked up several notches. We were always private about where we lived and where Z went to daycare. We never disclose the name of Zoomer's school on the blog or social media; we don't post pictures of Z in or near the school or mark it as a location where we are. We don't want people to know where our house is. My biggest fear is that someone will disagree with my parenting so strongly that they will take it upon themself to seek us out and take Zoomer from us.

I felt like I always had to have the house in perfect condition and hope Zoomer never had a tantrum in public. I felt like I had to prove how loved and healthy Zoomer is to people whose understanding of gender differs from mine. I was angry that anyone dared accuse me of child abuse because I use gender-neutral pronouns for my kid when there are literally children being kicked out of their homes or worse, murdered by their parents, because they are gay or trans.

We began taking extra precautions. We put wooden dowels in every window of our house. We installed security cameras. We put a chain on the interior of the front door—partly to keep intruders out and partly to keep Zoomer in after they learned how to open the front door, and, on one occasion, we found them on the front patio in their pajamas.

I talked to the directors of Zoomer's school. I told Robin I was scared. She had been following the story and tracking where it went.

Robin told me, "We've already been taking measures to protect Zoomer."

My heart was breaking during the entire conversation. I was angry that this whole thing had gotten so out of control and spread so far. I was angry at myself for not seeing this coming. I was angry that I felt like an ambassador for gender creative parenting, and I wanted more families to take on some of this public burden.

I stood in the office of Kid-Land, looking miserable, feeling defeated.

Robin told me, "I've told all our staff about what's going on. They know that if anyone asks if Zoomer goes here, they need to say no. We moved some things that have Zoomer's name on them so potential parents touring the facility won't see that they go here." I started crying. I felt like a terrible burden and terribly loved at the same time. Robin and all the staff at Kid-Land adored Zoomer and loved our family and were doing everything in their power to make sure we felt safe.

Things started to slow down after a few months. News stories didn't stop, but they became less frequent. Trolls who weren't getting the reaction out of me that they had hoped for lost interest and faded back into the garbage dump of the World Wide Web. It was truly like an eight-week storm lifted, and the sun came out again. I could focus on other things. I asked some friends in the Parenting Theybies Facebook group if any of them were interested in participating in the media game, and a few of them said they were willing to share their stories. I would pass on their names and email addresses to journalists looking for an interview. I wasn't interested in talking to every reporter, and I also wanted to help fellow gender creative parents get their stories out there. To diversify the stories, you must diversify the spokespeople.

So many friends from my online community stepped up and started doing interviews. Whether they were genuinely interested in talking with a reporter, or they were doing it out of compassion and to keep the movement growing, I'm forever grateful. Bobby McCullough continued doing interviews; Tiffany Cook, Ari Dennis, and others took on interviews. Kori Doty had been telling their story, and so had Jesi Taylor Cruz. Nate and Julia Sharpe did an interview with NBC in June, and one of my favorite resources for gender creative parenting is an interview Nate did with a radio station in Cambridge, Massachusetts.[25] I had felt alone, like I had been sitting on a stage all by myself under a bright, boiling spotlight for weeks, putting on a brave face, acting like everything was fine. Then all these other parents stepped into the light, and I was able to step off and recover.

The *MamaMia Out Loud* podcast[26] was that first podcast in Australia that Rachel had told us about, and in general, it was supportive of gender creative parenting. The hosts kind of came around more and more as they talked about it. They discussed scientific studies around how children are treated differently based on sex and presumed gender and unpacked their own assumptions in real time. I actually enjoyed listening to it, but I kept thinking about something that Mia Freedman, the creator of *MamaMia*, said in the podcast.

She said, regarding gender creative parents, "In your everyday life, you would have to have miniconfrontations with the people in your life daily. You would have to constantly reaffirm your position. All day every day, from the daycare to the supermarket to with the grandparents, you'd have to be having mini wars, and be on the defensive all the time."

This wasn't true for us, and it irked me that there might be someone in Sydney listening to the podcast and thinking, *Hey, I'd love to parent this way.* And then, after hearing the assumption that their life would be filled with mini wars all day every day, they might reconsider. I didn't feel compelled to contact every producer, journalist, and anchor to correct their inaccuracies about our family's experience, but I felt compelled to correct this one.

I clicked on Mia Freedman's Instagram account and sent her a direct message. I let her know that I heard the podcast and that I enjoyed it, and then I asked her for the opportunity to clear up some things that were said that I didn't think accurately reflected our reality, especially the parts that made it seem like a daily, stressful nightmare. She enthusiastically agreed and invited me for an interview on her podcast *No Filter*. Four months later, we Skyped and spoke for an hour. The podcast was released on August 26, 2018,[27] and it felt good to reclaim part of my story.

On February 13, 2019, almost a year into our story going global, I woke up and checked Instagram. There were mean comments from a few people. My blood pressure had certainly gone up after reading them, and my mood plummeted. I wasn't particularly upset about the comments as much as I was upset about the fact that I simply did not have any more time or energy to keep fighting these fights. Daily, the same type of comment, just from a different stranger, would pop up in the comment section, and I would feel like I had to address it immediately. That morning, something changed in me. I looked over at my gorgeous sleeping child, who had crawled into bed with us in the middle of the night, and thought, *You strangers don't get to rob any more of my time.* Maybe I'd get to it later; maybe I'd delete it; maybe one of our supporters would swoop in and try to defend us. I was tired of holding on to the feelings of strangers. The only thing I wanted to hold on to was this incredible little human in front of me who was growing up too quickly. I put my phone down and snuggled up to Zoomer. With their thumb in their mouth, and their eyes still closed, they said, "Hi, Mommy."

I smiled, letting the internet disappear, and said, "Good morning, Zoomie."

~

Stories about us and other gender creative families continue to be written. There are enough resources out there now that if someone was interested in parenting this way, a Google search would likely give them directions to us and hundreds of other resources created by and for people parenting this way.

It is an exhausting, overwhelming, bizarre experience being in the international spotlight. Seeing your child's photo in online news in a language you don't speak is jarring, to say the least. I am aware that a decision I made will now be a part of Zoomer's story and online presence forever. When Zoomer is older and they Google their name, they'll get more search results than an average teenager. I get that Zoomer will see the headlines from news sources all over the globe, from when they were a toddler being raised without an assigned gender, without expectations or limitations, when the world found that fascinating.

Yes, Zoomer's digital footprint started before they could walk, but I think Brent and I are parenting in a way that we are proud of, and we decided to share our story so that others could be inspired to do it too, if it resonated with them. I'm proud of the way Brent and I have handled it. We weathered a storm that most people will never experience; our parenting practices were on display for millions of people to criticize, and we came out on the other side with minor injuries, but intact. I hope Zoomer will understand that their parents love them unconditionally and made conscious decisions every single day so that they could grow up to be whoever they wanted to be and know they are accepted and supported.

I've had the great fortune to get to know families who decided to do gender creative parenting because of us. As Zoomer gets older, there will be more babies without assigned gender, more kids using they/them pronouns, and more public advocates for this way of parenting. There's a sea change happening, and I think Zoomer will come of age in a world that is more nonbinary than ever before. In 2031, as a fifteen-year-old, Zoomer will probably look back on 2018 and think, *Why was everyone making such a big deal about theybies?* And then they'll jump on their hoverboard and go hang out on the space station with their friends, who couldn't care less about gender.

SIXTEEN

Bangarang!

Brent and I decided early that we would let Zoomer's hair grow and just trim their fringe out of their eyes until Zoomer told us how they wanted their hair cut and styled. I started trimming their bangs when they were about eighteen months old and had to do a fresh fringe trim about every two to three months. I would sit Zoomer in their high chair and get their other hair out of the way with a clip or hair tie. Then I'd take Brent's beard-trimming scissors and cut Z's bangs so the fringe fell right above their eyebrows. This went well the first and second time I cut their bangs, when I was being a bit more cautious and conservative.

"I think Zoomer needs a fringe trim. Or should we try and grow it out?" I asked Brent one Saturday morning.

"Z hates hair clips at the moment, so I think it might be uncomfortable for them to have so much hair in their eyes all the time," Brent said. "We can see how it goes to grow their fringe out, though."

I nodded. "We'll let their fringe grow out."

Twenty minutes later, I put Zoomer in their high chair for lunch. Every time I looked at Zoomer, they were wiping their bangs out of their eyes with their grubby little food-covered hands. I grabbed a bobby pin and swooped their fringe to the side. Zoomer grabbed the bobby pin and took it out, leaving avocado in their hair like a styling gel.

"Forget it. I'm cutting your fringe," I said as I walked to the bathroom to get Brent's scissors.

Zoomer was working on their lunch with their head down, grabbing at some avocado. I scooped up their fringe in my hand and thought, *I'm going to go just a bit shorter this time so I don't have to do this again anytime soon.* I was standing in front of the high chair and making decisions with scissors while looking down at Zoomer's head. That was a mistake. I made a chop straight across that ended up being diagonal as the fringe shifted to the left as I cut from the right. I released their fringe from my fingers and their bangs fell back into place—except not really. They were uneven and comically too short.

"Oh noooo," I said in whispery horror. "This is not good!" I tried to assess this terrible haircut I had given my toddler.

"What happened?" Brent called from the living room.

I started laughing. It was so bad, but there was no remedy—time would be the only solution.

"I cut Zoomer's bangs, and it's not good."

Brent walked into the kitchen to look at the damage and said, "About a half hour ago, I thought we decided we were going to grow it out."

I nodded, my lips pursed. "Yeeeeah. I made an executive decision. And it didn't go well. Should I try and fix it?" I asked Brent.

Brent laughed. "No, I do not think you should keep going. You've done more than enough."

Zoomer looked up at us both, avocado on their face and the most jacked-up, choppy, crooked microfringe you've ever seen.

"I'm sorry, baby," I told them. "It will grow back."

I watched a fringe trimming tutorial on YouTube and made a trip to Sally Beauty. I got some proper hair-cutting supplies and a quick lesson from the nineteen-year-old behind the counter and vowed to improve my scissor skills.

It's unfair that bad haircuts take the longest time to grow out. The week after the bad fringe incident, I took Zoomer to California to visit an old friend from college and meet her kids for the first time. As we boarded the plane, a flight attendant got one look at Zoomer and said, "Looks like someone got ahold of the scissors."

I did some quick shame calculations. Did I want this flight attendant to think I let my two-year-old play with scissors, or did I want them to think I have no future in cosmetology? "Um, I actually cut their bangs. It's bad. I know. It's going to be fine. Kids are resilient," I said with a splattering of embarrassment. I found my seat near the back of the plane.

A couple of months later, when the media hoopla was happening, and thousands of people were visiting our Instagram account daily, people were commenting on pictures of Zoomer, saying, "Their parents don't even know how to cut hair properly!" and I laughed about it for days. They were so right. I learned a lot from that fringe trim and am looking forward to the day Zoomer tells us they want a haircut that is worth paying for, and I can retire from my kitchen-salon responsibilities.

I don't want Zoomer to grow up thinking short hair is "boy hair" and long hair is "girl hair." I just think hair should be hair, and people should do whatever they want to do with their own hair. Fortunately, Zoomer knows all types of people, with all types of genders, who have all types of hair, so they haven't been drawing any distinctions because there haven't been too many binary-gendered hair trends among the people in their world. In the first three years of their life, I had shoulder length hair, hair down the middle of my back, and then back up to chin length, and then very short hair.

I told Zoomer one Friday morning as they were leaving for school with Brent that I was going to get my hair cut. When I picked them up that afternoon, with my new do, they asked, "Where'd your hair go to?"

I told them, "I got it cut short. My long hair is probably in the garbage somewhere." I looked in the rearview mirror and said, "I look like Ryder from *PAW Patrol*. I'm liking it. Do you like it?"

Zoomer nodded and said, "Yeah, I like it."

Then I asked, "Zooms, do you want your hair cut?"

They shook their head, casually responded, "No," and carried on eating their goldfish crackers.

Zoomer liked having long hair but didn't really like having any hair accessories until after they turned three. We could occasionally get their bangs out of their eyes with an elastic or clip, and they went through a stage where they wanted Brent to give them a blow out after they got their hair washed. We were not above bribing Zoomer with M&M's to let us brush their hair when it was tangled. "Zoomer!" I pled. "Please let me brush your hair. You look like I found you in the forest!" Sometimes Zoomer looked a little feral, but they were happy, and that was more important to me.

As Zoomer gets older, I imagine they will be interested in cutting their hair into a new style, and although they seem to love their "lellow" hair, I imagine that someday Zoomer will want to experiment with new hair colors.

I began to think about creating resources for gender creative hair and had a perfect partner in mind. I invited my friend Emiley, a stylist at Lunatic Fringe in Salt Lake City who had been doing my hair for years, out for a drink. I had always loved the salon because it's an inclusive and safe space where a lot of incredible hair dreams come true. There were always queer and genderfluid stylists and clients in the salon, and everyone was complimenting each other on how wonderful they looked.

We sat at the bar at Water Witch and hatched a plan over cocktails. Emiley's job would be to recruit her stylists to volunteer their time for the day, and she would make the pitch to the owners of the salon and ask if they would donate the products that would be used for the event. I would work on finding models, and Brent would handle the photography.

With Emiley's help, we recruited twelve young models. Two-year-old Zoomer was the youngest, and the other models ranged in ages from three to seventeen. Ten stylists volunteered their time, and we all piled into Lunatic Fringe on a summer Sunday morning.

Before the young models arrived, I got to speak to all the stylists. We were standing in a circle, in between the salon stations and the chairs. I introduced myself.

"Hi, everyone. My name is Kyl. I am one of Emiley's clients, and she has become a great friend of mine. I have a two-year-old named Zoomer, who I didn't assign a gender to." Zoomer was standing next to me, leaning against my leg. I looked down at them and smiled. "We use they/them pronouns for Zoomer and try to make their world as gender expansive as possible and encourage Zoomer to simply be who they want to be." I ruffled Zoomer's hair a bit, and then they ran over to Brent, who was bringing photography equipment inside.

"I believe hair has a lot to do with personal expression, and I want there to be style guides for parents like me and kids like Zoomer to have for inspiration, which is why we are all here today. I want to say thank you. Thank you for coming in to work on your day off and volunteering your time to make this event happen. We have some really special kids coming in today. Some are cisgender, some are transgender, some are nonbinary, and I am so grateful that we get to create a space and give them a special day focused on what they want. Let me show you photos of the models and give you a little bit of information about them and what kind of hair they are interested in today."

I held my laptop in my hands and opened up the PowerPoint slides I had created. "This is Ayla. Ayla is four and wants a rainbow mullet." The stylists smiled, and all looked at Cole, who apparently is a mullet aficionado.

Cole said, "Oh yes! I'll take Ayla!"

I continued showing the photos, and the stylists quickly self-selected who would be the best match for each model.

After everyone knew who they would be spending the morning with, one of the stylists approached me. "I just want to say that I love what you are doing for Zoomer. I think it's amazing, and I'm so glad to be a part of this movement." We smiled at each other, and between us, four eyeballs got a little watery. After our moment of solidarity, I thanked him for being there, and we got absorbed by the bustle of the salon as the music was turned on, and the models and their parents arrived.

Kids jumped up into the black swivel salon chairs, with their parents standing by and some kids sitting in their parents' laps. The stylists crouched down to the eye level of their young models and said, "Talk to me about what you want to do with your hair today."

The kids had the most imaginative ideas and asked for them with confidence. "I want really short sides and longer blue hair on top," said one model.

"Yes! Let's do it!" said Stephen, their stylist.

Leo wanted fluorescent pink hair; Clover wanted hair like a horse; Zoe wanted cotton candy unicorn hair; and Emmy wanted a burgundy-colored, short, soft, feathered do. All the stylists got to work, washing, trimming, coloring, styling, while getting to know their young clients.

My friend Jess brought her three-year-old, Ida, and was graciously looking after Zoomer as I darted upstairs to get a photo release form from a parent and downstairs to help Brent set up the lights for the photo shoot. I paused and asked Zoomer, "Do you want anything done to your hair today? Do you want a color?"

Zoomer looked at me and said, "Yeah, pink hair, pwease."

Ida looked at Jess and said, "I want dinosaur hair!"

Just then, a stylist named Lara came by and said, "I will go get some hair extensions that these two can paint color on."

I left them to the activity and opened up bottles of Martinelli's sparkling cider and cans of La Croix. I poured them into small plastic cups and added some snacks to a tray, small containers of Pringles and small bags of fruit snacks. I wanted to make sure these kids felt special, like the stars they were. I walked around the salon like a flight attendant, offering the kids treats that they excitedly took and consumed, while draped in black capes and watching their stylists bring their imagination to life on their heads.

We took photos of the models alone and then some with their stylists and some with their parents. Afterward, everyone ate pizza together in the salon lobby, complimented each other's hair, and made the kids feel special and seen.

A few weeks later, after Brent did some design magic, we posted the Gender Creative Hair lookbook on raisingzoomer.com[28] and posted photos on Instagram with #GenderCreativeHair. Some of our followers started adding #GenderCreativeHair to photos of themselves and their cool kids.

Snuggled up on the couch one rainy afternoon, I showed the lookbook and hashtag to Zoomer, and they pointed to all the models and said, "I like their hair!"

I was proud of this thing that Brent, Emiley, and our community created. "I like their hair too!" I said. "And I like your hair, Zoomer!" I'll always tell Zoomer I like their hair.

A few months after Zoomer's third birthday, they got really into their hair. "I want T. rex hair!" they'd declare.

"Um. OK? Yeah. I know what that means. I'll give you T. rex hair." I found some hair elastics and put two little buns on the top of their head. "There. T. rex hair."

"Thank you, Mommy." Then they ran away with a "Raaawwwwwr!"

As their bangs started covering their eyes, Brent sat Zoomer down for a hair consultation.

"Sweetie, your fringe is starting to grow over your eyes again, and I worry about you having an accident because you can't see," Brent said. "You need to make a decision. You can either grow your fringe out, and you can pick out some clips or headbands that you like to keep it out of your eyes until you can tuck it behind your ears, or I can cut your fringe." Brent glanced over at me and smirked. "Because Mommy lost the right to come near your fringe with scissors."

Zoomer sat on the bench, genuinely weighing their options. "I want to grow it long."

"OK, let's go to Target, and you can pick out some clips," Brent said, scooping a tall Zoomie into his arms and walking down the stairs to get shoes on.

At Target, Brent put Zoomer in a cart and walked down the aisle with all the hair accessories, where packages of clips and poms and barrettes and scrunchies were displayed. "OK, sweetie, you can pick three packages," Brent said, leaning on the cart while Zoomer stood and looked at all their options.

"Those ones!" Zoomer exclaimed, pointing at a package of glittery rainbow snap clips.

Brent grabbed the clips off the hook and handed them to Zoomer. Zoomer gently placed them in the cart and then looked back at the display.

"The butterfly one," Zoomer said. Brent grabbed them and gave them to Zoomer.

"OK, Zoomer, what do you think about these rainbow scrunchies so we can put your hair in ponytails when you're on your bike?"

Zoomer looked at Brent. "They hurt?"

Brent read the package. "They say 'ouchless,' which means they shouldn't pull your hair."

Zoomer nodded in approval, reached their hands out, grabbed the package, and put it in the cart. On the way to the cash register, Zoomer slid a purple glittery butterfly clip out of the package and put it on their bangs.

"Daddy, can we go to the bike park now?" Zoomer asked.

"Yep, my little butterfly. Let's get you to the bike park," Brent replied.

And off our little lellow-haired kid went.

SEVENTEEN

Merfolk and Track Dreams

G ender stereotypes can be a self-fulfilling prophecy. Let's say a family has twins: one boy and one girl. If a parent thinks their infant son is more capable of physical activity than their daughter, then they may move their son around more and encourage his crawling and climbing more than they do for his sister. His muscles may gain strength, and he may gain confidence and skills earlier than his sister due to this unequal encouragement. After years of prioritizing their son's "need for activity," he is more athletic than his sister. "See? Boys are just faster," they'll say to their daughter, who did not receive the same physical upbringing as her brother.

It can be difficult to completely untangle what may or may not be a natural ability versus what was socially constructed and molded from infancy. In an enlightening study published in the *Journal of Experimental Child Psychology*, researchers conducted an experiment with a group of mothers and their eleven-month-old infants.[29] Half the babies were female, and half the babies were male (as reported by the mothers). For the experiment, the researchers set up a ramp with a platform on the top and netting on either side, and the researchers could change the incline of the ramp from fairly flat to relatively steep.

The researchers asked each mother to place their child on the platform. Then the researchers asked the mothers to estimate their children's crawling abilities at different inclines. Next, they let the babies crawl around on the platform and down the ramp with varying steepness.

Male and female babies showed identical levels of motor performance; what differed was their mothers' estimations of their crawling abilities. Mothers of girls *under*estimated their daughters' performance, and mothers of boys *over*estimated their sons' performance. Many of the physical, emotional, and verbal differences we see between boys and girls are largely socially constructed and reinforced through stereotypes.

If we want our children to grow up believing that men and women are equal, we need to treat them as equals in childhood. If we want children to grow up outside the constraints of boy = masculinity and girl = femininity, then we need to provide room for children to explore their interests without gendered boundaries.

Some girls may be more interested in playing football than cheerleading on the sidelines. Some boys may give zero shits about sports and be more interested in art or baking or fashion—and some boys may love sports *and* cosmetics. We have to stop putting kids in categories of interest before we understand their actual interests.

While our family was on vacation in Florida, I was looking over the daily activities offered by the resort. "Swim class!" *Oooh, fun!* I thought. The flyer went on: "Girls will use mermaid tails and boys will use shark fins." As I sat on the crisp white duvet of the hotel bed, my eyes rolled to the back of my head. *Can't it just say, "Kids can choose from merfolk tails and shark fins in this fun class"? Can we just stop for one second while creating kids' classes and think to ourselves, "Hmm . . . there might be boys who want to be a merboy, and there might be girls whose favorite animal is a shark because* shocker! *There are female sharks in the ocean. So why don't we just put the tails and fins out and let kids choose their own adventure?* While my internal thoughts might land on more of the feisty side, my external suggestions always come from a kind place with a loving tone because that's how I tend to have more success.

No one wants to be reprimanded for what they consider an action that came from a good place without any malice behind it. I don't think that the program director at the Hilton in Orlando was thinking, *All these little overachieving, assertive girls, trying to abandon their innate, God-given role of sexy mermaid; not a chance I'm letting them be a badass shark!* I just think stereotypes are so deeply embedded in our unconscious minds that, if we aren't careful, we might make choices that perpetuate bias.

Our family didn't go to the class, not because of the gendered shark/mermaid binary, but because Zoomer was two and couldn't swim yet, and we were going to Disney World that day. I left that battle to another progressive, feminist parent or to a boy who would say, "Screw your binary" while he slipped into a fabulous, shiny tail.

~

Track meets were a big deal in my house growing up. The Myers kids were quick and competitive. I looked forward to the annual community track meet every year with Christmas-like anticipation.

My parents bought us Aqua Socks from Kmart, the "water shoes" that come in different neon-colored mesh. We were convinced that they were our secret weapon, making us lighter and more aerodynamic than the other elementary school kids. In hindsight, though, the real reason we wore them is probably because they were $8.99 and were a much more affordable alternative to buying Nike shoes for three quickly growing kids.

A year before I got pregnant, I noticed a "Young Sprints Track Meet" banner fastened to the chain-link fence surrounding the local high school's football stadium and track. Memories from the Oregon track meets we frequented in the '90s came flooding back. My mom would pack a cooler of peanut butter and jelly sandwiches, orange slices, and Gatorade. My dad would fill our orange two-gallon sports jug with ice water. I'd pick out a lime-green scrunchie to match my water shoes, and we'd load into our Dodge Caravan with wood paneling and head to the high school track to sprint a hundred meters and get a wicked sunburn. *Young Sprints track meet!* I thought to myself, *I can't wait till I have a little one who can run in that!*

The following June, I had a fertilized egg implanting in my uterus. Blastocyst Zoomer couldn't run in the 2015 track meet. The year after that, Zoomer was three months old, and there weren't any Aqua Socks their size, so we had to pass on the 2016 Young Sprints meet. In 2017, Zoomer was nine months short of the qualifying age of two, so we reassured them that next year—2018—was *their* year. On a hot summer day in 2018, while driving home from work, I saw it . . . the banner: "Young Sprints Track Meet—June 5!" I called Brent immediately.

"The Young Sprints track meet is next Tuesday. We're doin' it!" I said.

"OK," Brent said, probably still working on his laptop.

"You don't seem nearly as excited as I am," I accused.

"I'm probably not. But I'm so happy you are excited," Brent replied.

"I'll send you a calendar invite, love you, bye."

Zoomer was living up to their name and becoming a very quick kid. They loved to run and were constantly yelling, "Chase me!" to anyone who would listen. I figured we would try out the track meet and see if they liked running in a lane, or if free-range grass running was more their style.

The track meet was on a Tuesday evening. I left work early, picked Zoomer up, and took them home to get prepared. We filled up water bottles and got our hair out of our faces. We got our shorts and T-shirts on and slipped our fast feet into socks and sneakers, or "running thooth" as Zoomer called them. Brent got home and changed, and we piled into the car and swung by Little Caesars to grab a pizza. There was no time to lose; we needed to get to that track.

The day before the meet, I looked over the promotional flyer. Nothing suggested the track meet would be gendered—why would it be? The divisions ranged from ages two through ten; virtually all the participants would be prepubescent. It was all just for fun. We got to the track, and I filled out the form.

Child's name: Zoomer Courtney-Myers

Guardian: Kyl Myers

Do you understand that we have no liability if your kid wipes out and breaks all the bones in their body? (I'm paraphrasing): Yep.

Gender: [left blank]

I handed the form to the volunteer taking the money.

"Are the events going to be segregated by gender?" I asked.

"No," they kindly responded as they gave me change for a twenty.

I signed Zoomer up for the fifty-meter dash, one-hundred-meter dash, softball throw, and hurdles.

"Hurdles?" I laughed. "How will a two-year-old clear a hurdle?" I asked the volunteer.

They pointed across the track with their pen, and I followed their cue. A row of hurdles made out of PVC pipe and the height of croquet wickets were propped up on the track next to the long jump.

"Get the hell out of here. How could you possibly make something so cute?" I exclaimed. We chuckled. *Hurdles*, I said under my breath, shaking my head, basking in the adorableness of it all.

We got ourselves situated in the stands and carb loaded with a slice of cheese pizza. The Young Sprints track meet got kicked off with an all-ages, all-gender race walk. We belly laughed as kids tried their hardest to make their way around the track, keeping one foot down at all times. *This is great*, I thought. *Kids are just running together. I love it.*

Over the loudspeaker, the announcer called for all the two- and three-year-olds to come down to the track for the fifty-meter race.

I looked at Zoomer and said, "That's you! It's your turn to run!"

Zoomer was excited and said, "Zoomer running!"

We stood up and made our way down the metal bleachers and onto the track. As we approached the grassy area near the starting line, I heard one of the organizers saying, "Two- and three-year-old boys in this line; two- and three-year-old girls in this line." I froze. I was shocked that the children, *the toddlers*, were being separated by gender. I thought about asking the organizer where Zoomer would go—who hasn't told me their gender. I thought about asking the organizer to not do this, to just let the kids run together. I thought about just letting Zoomer pick a line.

I said, "You're separating the kids? This should not be gender segregated." The organizer didn't seem to hear me. Things were happening quickly, and I didn't know what to do. All I could think was, *We're not doing this.*

Brent had been standing near the finish line, ready to take photos of Zoomer running their race. He watched as I walked out of the crowd with Zoomer on my hip. Brent jogged over to us, "Are they separating boys and girls?" he asked.

I nodded. I felt so sad and deflated. "They are having boys line up in one line and girls in another and then doing heats by gender. I stood there for thirty seconds, thinking through my options." I shook my head. "I can't do this. I'm not going to have Zoomer choose a line. The organizers are too busy to stop and reconsider. Why am I the only parent who didn't think that was OK?"

Brent was frowning. "You did the right thing, Kyl. I'm so sorry, though. I know how excited you were for this."

"Will you take Zoomer and go get our stuff? I'm going to go get our money back," I told him. Brent held his arms out, Zoomer climbed into them, and they headed toward the bleachers.

I walked to the registration table, and the same person who had taken my money and told me the events wouldn't be gender segregated smiled at me and asked what I needed.

I said, "I was under the impression that this would not be a gender-segregated event."

The volunteer said, "Oh. Are they separating the kids?"

"They are, and I'm not going to put my child in one line and make them feel different than other children. We were really excited about this, but I don't think it's right to make toddlers run different races according to gender. I'd like to have my money back."

The volunteer gave me a ten-dollar bill and said, "I'm sorry. I didn't realize they were going to separate the kids."

"I'm sorry too. I hope you'll remind them to do better next year."

I walked out of the track meet and cried. I was so disappointed that toddlers and preschoolers were being separated by gender. For what? It is these types of moments that plant the seeds that boys and girls are dramatically different, and in the case of track and field, that boys are better.

I tried to hide my tears from Zoomer as Brent got them in their car seat, and I sat in the front. Brent put our pizza box and bag of belongings in the back of the car and then got in on the driver's side. I took a few deep breaths. I didn't want to talk about this in front of Zoomer.

"Want to go to Liberty Park?" I asked Brent.

"Mmhmm," Brent affirmed as he put his hand on my leg to comfort me.

"I not running?" Zoomer asked from the back seat.

I felt terrible for leaving. Zoomer just wanted to run. But I also would have felt terrible if I had stayed, complicit in perpetuating the binary system that I was working so hard to dismantle.

Brent responded to Zoomer in a chipper voice. "Honey, we are going to go to Liberty Park, and you are going to race Mommy and Daddy! Does that sound fun?"

Zoomer threw their hands in the air. "Yeah!" they exclaimed, and then, in a cheeky voice, they said, "I gonna wiiin." I felt relieved that

Zoomer wasn't feeling upset that we left the track meet. At least not as upset as I was.

My sister Storie met us at the park. We got out of the car and made our way over to the playground. Brent was holding the pizza box and said, "I'm ready to run!" Brent, Zoomer, and Storie stood at an imaginary starting line while I ran down the sidewalk to an imaginary finish line.

"Are you ready to race?" I called out.

The contestants all shouted, *"Yeah!"*

I stood on the sidewalk twenty meters from them and yelled, "On your mark! Get set! Go!"

The racers started running toward me. Brent and I looked at each other and laughed, both realizing how fast Zoomer actually was. Their little arms were pumping, and they had a determined look on their face as they sprinted toward me. I knelt down on the ground and opened my arms up, and Zoomer was absorbed into my embrace.

Brent was right behind them. "Zoomer! You won! You're so quick!"

Zoomer was beaming.

"When you catch your breath, will you race me?" I asked.

Zoomer nodded enthusiastically and said, "Yes, I race you, Mommy."

We played on the playground, swinging on monkey bars and sliding down slides. We had mini races: who could run to the tree first, who could run to Daddy first. It wasn't the track meet I had planned on, but it was the inclusive track meet I was looking for.

~

I want more feminists to see the gross inequalities in all these everyday gender segregations between boys and girls. I want more feminists to step up and say, "Nope, not on my watch!" I want more feminists to realize that by going along with sex-segregated activities—where no one is using genitals to participate—they are complicit in perpetuating gender stereotypes and inequalities.

It probably comes as no surprise that I seek out activities where children are combined into the same class and things aren't based on being a "boy" or a "girl." If getting into two or more lines is absolutely necessary, I encourage people to have kids line up based on anything other than gender. Have kids line up by spring and summer birthdays and fall and winter birthdays; have an "I like apple juice more" line and an "I like orange juice more" line. Extracurricular activities that don't categorize by gender are more powerful than people give credit for. They help teach children that they'll be playing, learning, and working together for the rest of their lives, so let's embrace diversity and inclusion right now.

I emailed the board of directors of the Young Sprints track meet. I let them know we were there and why we left. I kindly asked them to not separate girls and boys at next year's track meet and gave some explanations why. A couple of days later, the board chair responded to me and said that my email had generated a great deal of conversation among the board members. They thanked me for bringing this concern to their attention, and they said they would be taking my recommendations under consideration for next year's Young Sprints track meet, where they would work to ensure every child felt welcomed and encouraged to participate.

A year later, I was driving to pick up Zoomer from school after work. I passed the high school track and field and saw people setting up for an event. *I bet that's the Young Sprints track meet,* I thought to myself. On the chain-link fence there was a banner: "Young Sprints Track Meet, June 4, 5:15 p.m." *That's today.*

I looked at the clock on my dashboard. It was almost 5:00 p.m. Brent was in Phoenix for work. Some friends were coming over to our house for dinner with Zoomer and me in a half hour. The 2019 Young Sprints track meet wasn't in the cards for the Courtney-Myers family. I hoped they had taken my feedback on board. I hoped that this year would be a little different than the last.

The day after the track meet that we didn't attend, Zoomer, Brent, and I went to watch an end-of-year jazz band concert that our family friend was performing in. As we approached the audience of supporters looking toward a stage of adolescent musicians, our friend Tracy spotted us and emerged from the crowd.

We hadn't seen each other in a couple of years, and as we were catching up, a young kid with shoulder-length brown hair, a pink shirt with a snow cone on it, galaxy-print leggings, and sparkly fuchsia slip-on shoes ran up and stood next to Tracy. I looked at the child for a moment before realizing who they were.

"Arrow?" I asked with excitement. He'd grown up so much since the last time I saw him.

"Yep!" His smile had a new set of teeth pushing through the gums where his baby teeth used to be.

"How old are you now?" I asked.

"I'm seven," he replied in a bubbly voice.

I shook my head in disbelief. It seemed like yesterday I was babysitting him when he was an infant.

"My mom told me that you were frustrated with the Young Sprints track meet," Arrow said matter-of-factly.

I smiled and glanced at Tracy. Tracy ruffled Arrow's hair. "Some conversations are meant to stay in the car, Arrow."

"It's OK," I reassured Tracy. "Yeah, Arrow, I was frustrated last year when they were separating the boys and the girls for the races," I said. Then I remembered the track meet was last night. "Did you go to the track meet yesterday?" I asked.

Arrow nodded. "Want to see the video of me running the hundred-meter dash? I won."

"Of course you won. And of course I want to see the video," I replied.

As Arrow fiddled with his mom's phone to find the video, I looked up at Tracy and asked, "Did they separate the kids by gender?"

Tracy nodded and rolled her eyes. "Yeah."

In that moment, I felt grateful I hadn't gone last night but also disappointed that my complaint last year didn't make any difference.

Arrow looked up at me. "The boys kept telling me I was in the wrong line because I look like a girl. They told me I couldn't run with them because I have long hair. One of them shoved me."

I looked down at this beautiful, confident, resilient, gender-fluid child, heartbroken that he had been bullied for being himself. Angry that instances like that could be avoided if events were explicitly more inclusive. The exact thing that I had warned the board about had happened.

"Arrow, I am so sorry that happened to you. It's too bad those kids didn't take the time to get to know you, because you are awesome. I think your hair is great. And look at me. I'm a girl, and I have short hair. Hair doesn't have gender; you get to do whatever feels good for you." I smiled at Arrow. "Now, you said all those kids ate your dust, right? Show me that video."

Arrow showed me the videos of him smoking the other boys in the fifty- and hundred-meter races and the hurdles event and said, "I'm fast like lightning like the Flash." I nodded in agreement. Arrow added, "And I'm a great dresser, like Wonder Woman."

I smiled. "That you are, Arrow."

You win some, and you lose some. I wish the Young Sprints board had heeded my advice and done away with gender-segregated races. I wish Arrow could have enjoyed the event without being made to feel like he didn't belong. I wish more children were growing up learning that gender identities and expressions are diverse, and that's a good thing.

The Young Sprints event organizers haven't caught up to this movement yet. This movement that is leaving stereotypes and unnecessary categories behind. One day, they'll wake up and recognize they've been left in the sparkly dust and that it's in their best interest to sprint toward equality. Until then, I think I've got a gender creative track meet to organize.

EIGHTEEN

Harvey Milk Boulevard

I didn't know any out queer people when I was growing up. For most of my childhood and adolescence, I hadn't heard a single thing about gay or lesbian folks. My parents didn't have gay friends or seem to have any opinions about the matter. While I never heard my parents utter anything antigay, I also didn't hear anything that suggested they were allies, and they certainly didn't act like they believed there was a possibility one (or more) of their kids would be queer.

I was a girl, happily attracted to boys, and oblivious to the idea that I could also be attracted to girls or nonbinary people. Once, when I was sixteen and watching a Backstreet Boys music video on MTV, my dad walked into the living room and said, "I'd go gay for that Kevin one." We laughed, and that was it. That was the one interaction with my dad in which I determined he was on the ally side of gay issues. Not that I knew anything about gay issues.

By my early twenties, I realized that I was attracted to women as well as men, and then, when I was twenty-four, I started dating Reese, who was genderqueer. When I told my mom I was bisexual, she just said, "OK, are you dating someone?" and I told her about Reese.

I sent an email to my dad and his wife, April, to let them know I was bisexual. I was too terrified to tell them in person or over the phone. I wish I could remember what the subject line of that email was. "I'm coming out!" Or was it "Hi! I'm Bi!" My dad didn't reply to my email, but he didn't treat me any differently either after I knew he had received it. That's his style, though. He's a don't-rock-the-boat nice guy.

I didn't realize at the time that my sexual identity would evolve from bisexual to pansexual, and around the age of twenty-six, I would decide the word *queer* fit me best. As I was discovering my own sexuality, I was also discovering the queer community in Salt Lake City and got to be a part of the big, affirming changes happening in the state of Utah.

I met Derek Kitchen in 2011, during a study abroad program in Oviedo, Spain. After an intensive week of Spanish classes, a hundred students from Utah would go on organized excursions every weekend. One excursion was a kayaking trip, and Derek asked if I'd like to be his partner.

Derek smoothed sunscreen on his fair arms and legs and on his face and ears before putting his hat back on over his red hair. "Do you want some sunscreen?" he asked me.

"Nah, not yet. I'm gonna let this Spanish sun bronze me for a while." We smiled at each other and put our life jackets on before pushing the kayak in the river and climbing in.

As we floated, Derek and I discussed relationships, family, and our goals. Derek told me about his partner, Moudi, and I told Derek about my love for the single life and how I was trying to figure out my own sexual identity. We were vulnerable with one another and allowed each other in.

In spring of 2013, Derek and Moudi were one of three same-sex couples who brought a suit against the state of Utah in the *Kitchen v. Herbert* case, suing on grounds that the prohibition of same-sex marriage in Utah was unconstitutional. Suing the state takes a while, as

I had learned with Prop 8 in California, and there was a long wait between when Derek's suit was filed on March 25 and when arguments were heard on December 4. Throughout the changes of seasons, from spring to summer, fall, and winter, Derek stayed confident and hopeful, knowing he was doing the right thing. During the last week of November, Derek called me.

"Do you want to come to the district court on Wednesday? The judge is hearing arguments on the case, and I'd love if you were there." I knew I had to be there.

I stood outside and watched as Derek, Moudi, their lawyer, and the two other couples walked into the courthouse while news crews took photos and filmed. People filed into a grandiose courtroom and waited for the Honorable Judge Robert J. Shelby to arrive. It was standing room only, with the majority of the audience supporting the plaintiffs. After the arguments were made, Judge Shelby thanked the attorneys and adjourned with a quick pound of the gavel. And now, all we could do was wait.

Any news? I asked Derek in a text a week later.

Not yet. But we think he's going to make a decision before the holidays, Derek responded. Derek knew so much more than I did about how this process would go. He gave me a *Schoolhouse Rock!*–type lesson on stays and appeals and assured me that waiting was just part of the process. Derek was wise beyond his years, incredibly intelligent—both intellectually and emotionally—and also calculated, humble, and compassionate. He would be a great policymaker, I thought—which he would go on to do as a Salt Lake City council member and then a Utah state senator.

On December 20, 2013, Judge Shelby ruled in favor of the plaintiffs, and same-sex marriage was legal in Utah . . . for a little while. The lawyers who represented the state hadn't filed the routine paperwork requesting a stay of proceedings in case the state lost. Without a filed stay from the state, the judge's decision that banning same-sex marriage was unconstitutional, and same-sex couples should be allowed to marry in Utah, became law immediately. During a seventeen-day window, more than twelve hundred couples rushed to county clerk's offices in twenty-two counties across the state of Utah to get marriage licenses. Washington County in southern Utah, the conservative place where I grew up and my family still lived, was no exception. On December 21, I got a call from my dad, the Honorable Judge Karlin S. Myers.

"Hi, honey. My office has been receiving a lot of calls from couples who want to get married. Apparently, many of the other judges down here in southern Utah won't marry them because they aren't sure about the law yet. I've read the decision. Same-sex marriage is legal in Utah, and I'm happy to marry these couples, and I have a bunch of ceremonies scheduled for this week."

I was grinning from ear to ear. "That's great, Dad. I'm so happy to hear you're helping people get married."

He continued, "I'm wondering if you want to come down and be a witness for these marriages and help sign the marriage certificates?"

I choked up.

"Of course. I'll head down tomorrow. Thanks for thinking of me, Dad."

"I'm always thinking of you, Kylee."

I walked into my dad's courtroom in Hurricane, Utah, a small rural city, twenty-three miles from Zion National Park. The first marriage my dad officiated was between two women. They stood in T-shirts and jeans, with their two young children leaning against their legs. My dad went through the exact script he had for hundreds of marriages between women and men, flawlessly replacing words to describe the same-sex couple before him. He used *partner* and *spouse* and *wife* for both women without skipping a beat. The only moment he got awkward was at the very end when he said, "You can now kiss . . . if you want." I made a mental note to mention this to him before the next ceremony. The couple hadn't brought anyone with them, so my dad's court clerk and

I signed as witnesses on their marriage certificate. Two men were in the court's lobby, waiting to get married next.

"Hey, Dad . . . ," I started. We were alone in the courtroom.

"Yeah, honey?" My dad was looking at me and smiling, realizing how good it feels to be a progressive ally, on the right side of history.

"I noticed that you said, 'You can now kiss if you want' to that couple. Dad . . . they're getting married. They want to smooch. Drop the 'if you want.'"

My dad laughed. "Yeah, I don't know why I did that. Got it!"

Before his court closed for the holiday, my dad married a few more same-sex couples that day, with his queer daughter smiling in the gallery.

The state filed a stay, and Utah had a story similar to California's, with the case moving up the court system hierarchy with appeals and affirmed decisions until October 2014, when the Supreme Court denied the state's petition. Same-sex couples could get married in Utah. And in June 2015 the US Supreme Court struck down all state bans on same-sex marriage and legalized it in all fifty states.

Derek and Moudi, being *the* gay couple of Utah, planned an incredible wedding at the Gallivan Center, a public space in downtown Salt Lake, and invited everyone. Literally. The wedding was open to the public. They were surrounded by their friends and family and thousands of supporters who were grateful for what they did to pave the way for marriage equality. Brent and I were proudly in the audience as Derek and Moudi became husband and husband.

~

When Zoomer was almost three years old, my friend Tara invited us to be the witnesses at her and Denelle's marriage ceremony at the Salt Lake county building in late December.

Zoomer sat on a chair between Brent and me. They were holding a small wooden box that had Tara and Denelle's rings in it.

"What's these?" Zoomer asked.

"Those are Tara and Denelle's wedding rings. Tara and Denelle are getting married today," I told Zoomer.

"What's married?" Zoomer asked.

"Some people choose to get married when they love each other. Mommy and Daddy love each other and are married. And Tara and Denelle love each other and are going to get married."

Zoomer was looking at me; their toddler brain didn't quite understand romantic love and marriage yet.

Jokingly, I added, "Mainly getting married is helpful for taxes and health insurance."

Brent laughed and shook his head.

Zoomer did a slow blink and asked, "What's taxes?"

I ran my fingers through Zoomer's long, coppery-colored hair and said, "Nothing you need to worry about just yet."

Tara told us it was time, and the five of us followed a county employee who had put a black robe over her jeans and sweater into a small room with a few chairs and a winter holiday wreath. The marriage ceremony was short and sweet and the first ceremony Zoomer had been a part of.

On Zoomer's second birthday, we went to Weller Book Works, a local bookshop in Salt Lake City, to buy Z a new book. We're typically a public library family, so every month we fill up a bag with five to ten books to borrow and read for a few weeks, return, and repeat the process. I don't buy books often, so when I do, I try to be intentional and use my money to support someone who is creating something that I think the world could use more of. We spent some time browsing the shelves, bypassing the hyper-gendered books that smelled like stereotypes. And then I came across *Harriet Gets Carried Away* by Jessie Sima.

I sat down on a bench and opened it up. Harriet is a young kid who lives in New York City and wears costumes every single day. In the story, it's Harriet's birthday, and her dads and Harriet head to the store to get the final necessities for her party. While at the store, Harriet meets some new friends and gets carried away on an adventure and has to find her way back home. It's a cute story with adorable illustrations. I liked that Harriet was an adventurous little kid and that she had two dads. I showed the book to Brent and Zoomer, and they both agreed it was a great book to buy for Z's birthday.

That night, Zoomer and I snuggled up in bed, and I read the book to them. Zoomer pointed to Harriet's dads on one of the pages and said, "Two daddies."

I looked at Zoomer and said, "Yep, Harriet has two dads."

Zoomer looked at me and asked, "Zoomie hab two dads?"

I told them, "You have one daddy and one mommy. Some kids have two mommies, and some kids have two daddies. Some kids have a mapa or an amma or a zaza, or their parent goes by another name. Some people live with their grandparents. There are all types of families."

Zoomer nodded and said, "Oh, OK."

I'm trying to build something new for Zoomer, a world where everything is for everyone, and everyone is loved. I feel lucky to have family, friends, community, courts, and authors helping me in this process.

Just a few weeks after Zoomer was born, Brent and I got Zoomer in their car seat, and we made our way to the City Building, where the Salt Lake City Council would be deciding on changing the name of 900 South to Harvey Milk Boulevard. I didn't know who Harvey Milk was until the 2008 film *Milk* came out. And now I joined hundreds of other residents in the standing-room-only chambers, there to show support for the street name change, proud to have a street named after a person who did so much for the gay rights movement. We were all there to say, "Salt Lake City is a place where everyone is welcome" and "Love is Love." I sat on a bench in the back. Brent stood behind me, holding Zoomer. We both looked on as our friend, Council Member Derek Kitchen, voted for the name change, and every other council member followed suit. It was official. Salt Lake City had a street named after Harvey Milk.

A month later, the city threw a Dedication Day party on the corner of 900 East and 900 South—the new Harvey Milk Boulevard. On a hot day in the middle of May, I got Zoomer dressed in a little tank-top onesie. It was light gray with big blue polka dots. Brent got Zoomer's diaper bag loaded up with all the essentials for a day out. We put Zoomer in the stroller and walked to the party.

On a stage in the middle of a closed intersection, the director of Equality Utah spoke about the significance of this dedication. Jackie Biskupski, the mayor of Salt Lake City, remarked how it was because of Harvey Milk that she was able to serve as an openly gay mayor. Tyler Glenn from Neon Trees sang songs as people danced and hugged and celebrated a wonderful day of inclusion, acceptance, and love.

Under the stop signs, for miles, brand-new green street signs were installed, with the words "Harvey Milk Boulevard." I was holding Zoomer and drinking an iced coffee under the shade of a huge tree when I noticed the sign. "Brent, will you take a picture of us, please?" I handed Brent my phone and got situated. The photo is of me, holding Zoomer in the air. Right above them is the green Harvey Milk Boulevard street sign. I'm looking up at Zoomer, and Zoomer is looking toward the party with a little smile on their eight-week-old face.

I don't get too caught up imagining hypothetical situations in the future. I don't pretend to have any idea what Zoomer's romantic life will look like as they get older. Brent and I are striving to create an environment where Zoomer learns that all sexualities and relationships between consenting people should be celebrated. There are no default assumptions. Brent and I simply hope Zoomer will feel comfortable bringing anyone they like, lust, or love into our home.

If I did have to imagine our life ten years from now, I see our home being a safe place, a refuge for kids who need a space where they can be themselves. I imagine regularly cooking dinner for half a dozen kids and calling out to Zoomer and their friends that food is ready. I imagine sitting around the table and being schooled on all the terminology that Generation Alpha, the children of Millennials, use to describe their relationships and sexual identities. I imagine myself grabbing a clean towel out of the closet for one of Zoomer's friends who just came out as queer, doesn't feel safe at home, and is staying with us for a few days. I imagine myself hugging teenagers and telling them that they are perfect just the way they are.

I'll tell Zoomer and their friends that I am queer. I'll tell them that Grandpa Myers is into Kevin from the Backstreet Boys and was one of the first judges in Utah to officiate same-sex marriages. I'll point out the Harvey Milk Boulevard sign when Zoomer is older, and I'll tell them who Harvey Milk was and that Zoomer was the youngest person in the room when the city council voted on naming a street after him. We'll keep having family dinners with Tara and Denelle and going on adventures with Uncle Derek. We'll continue reading stories about queer families, watching *Queer Kids' Stuff*, and supporting queer artists and plaintiffs. Maybe Zoomer will be queer; maybe they'll be straight; maybe they'll identify with a term I haven't heard yet. What I know for sure is Zoomer will know they are unconditionally loved.

NINETEEN

A Weekend in Moab

On Presidents' Day weekend, the Courtney-Myers trio piled into the car for our second annual trip to Moab, Utah, just one month shy of Zoomer's third birthday. I had been working long hours over the last few months, and I was desperate for a vacation, but I was mostly looking forward to three whole days of quality family time with Zoomer and Brent. We didn't have many plans for the weekend. We hoped to hike a little bit, visit Moab Giants, eat, hot tub, relax, and repeat. What I definitely hadn't planned on was having my heart explode all over the place for seventy-two hours.

After a four-hour drive and a dinner stop at a fast-food restaurant, we made it to our hotel in Moab around 8:00 p.m. on Friday. Exhausted from a long week, Brent and I made ourselves at home in room 220; we changed into pajamas, and both of us sprawled out like starfish on the two queen beds. Zoomer climbed into bed with Brent and snuggled up. We watched half an episode of *Diners, Drive-Ins and Dives*, and all of us conked out before nine.

The next morning, I had the TV on in the room while we were getting ready to go to Moab Giants, an interactive park with life-size dinosaurs. An advertisement for an eczema medication came on. The main actor, who I had assumed was a woman, was itching and scratching and looking uncomfortable. Zoomer stopped building their fort of pillows, looked at the screen, and asked, "What they doing? They OK?" then looked to me for answers.

Pleasantly surprised by their use of a gender-neutral pronoun for someone they didn't know, I smiled and said, "They have eczema, like you, and their skin can feel itchy, so they are using some medicine to feel better."

Zoomer nodded; said "Oh," satisfied; and returned to their activity, collecting every pillow in our room.

Although Zoomer opts to use first names more than pronouns, I hear Zoomer use *she* and *he* pronouns for their friends and teachers, sometimes getting the pronoun right, but not always. I don't know exactly how Zoomer understands pronouns at this point. Of course, they hear gendered pronouns being used all day long. At school, they are exposed to more she/her and he/him pronouns than anywhere else. Zoomer hears people use *they/them* when talking about Zoomer. I always try to use they/them pronouns for everyone until I know what pronouns they use for themself.

I use the correct pronoun for a person in response to Zoomer. Zoomer will say, "Where Daddy go? I miss her?"

I'll say, "I miss him too. He'll be home soon." We're starting to enter the stage where we can teach Zoomer that pronouns are shortcuts when we talk about someone, and different people use different pronouns, and it's best to ask which pronouns someone would like us to use for them.

After a full day of adventuring and hiking, we had dinner at a sushi restaurant and then walked back to our hotel.

"We go in the hot tub?" Zoomer excitedly asked as we made our way into the hotel lobby.

"Yeah! Let's go in the hot tub! Let's see if the hotel has a swim diaper."

Zoomer and I walked over to the gift shop and grabbed a Little Swimmer diaper and a pack of Starbursts. Zoomer ran up the stairs and down the hall to our room, with a diaper in one hand and the candy in the other. They bounced up and down excitedly until I unlocked the door. In the room, they started kicking their shoes off and trying to take their shirt off.

"I'll help you, sweetie," I said as I lifted Zoomer's shirt over their head. "Lie down and I'll put your swim diaper on."

Zoomer kept repeating, "We're going to the hot tub!" in their sing-songy voice.

"That's right, honey, we're going to the hot tub."

Brent was on the bed with a box of tissues, not feeling great. He decided to stay in the room. I put my swimsuit on, and Zoomer and I set out on the hunt for the hot tub.

After giving Zoomie a quick ride on the hotel's luggage cart, we discovered the pool area. There were two hot tubs. A bigger, longer one that had a little waterfall into a smaller circular hot tub below it. There was a couple in the upper hot tub, probably in their late sixties. I said hello and asked how their day was. They told me about their hike in Arches National Park, and I told them about the dinosaurs at Moab Giants. Zoomie and I stepped into the lower hot tub and out of sight of the couple. We pretended to be dinosaurs, like the ones we'd seen earlier. And then Zoomer said, "Mommy, be a zombie!"

I laughed. "Where did you hear about zombies?"

Zoomer put their arms straight in front of them, squinted their eyes, made a growly sound, and walked along the hot tub bench. "Like that mommy. That a zombie." I laughed again and did as instructed. I mommy-zombied toward them as they squealed.

"Let's make some food!" Zoomer declared.

"OK! What would you like to make?"

Predictably, they asked for macaroni and cheese.

"What kind of macaroni and cheese would you like?" I asked Zoomer, my lone customer in my imaginary hot tub restaurant.

"I want blueberries in it," they started. "And . . . and . . . and . . . french fries and ice cream and toast."

I whipped up their order and presented it to them, "Here you go, enjoy!"

When it was my turn to order and Zoomer's turn to cook, I asked for a sandwich with macaroni and cheese and lobster. They looked around in the hot tub and then up at me and, with all seriousness, said, "We all sold out."

I laughed. "Your imaginary restaurant, where you can literally imagine that you have anything, is all sold out of mac and cheese lobster sandwiches?"

Zoomer had a solemn look on their face. "Yeah, we all sold out."

I couldn't believe that this incredible child was all mine, and I got to spend as much time with them as I wanted. "Well, I'll have whatever you recommend." I relented. And my tiny little chef made me an imaginary "green smoovie wif rafberrieth."

Another hotel guest walked into the pool area and, before getting into the hot tub, asked if we'd mind if the jets were on. "No, not at all. Go for it!" I said. With a turn of the dial, the jets in the tub roared to life, and Zoomie and I were in a bubbling cauldron.

There was lots of reminding Zoomer to watch out where they were stepping, to keep their head above the water, and to sit on the edge of the hot tub every few minutes to cool off.

Zoomer kept saying, "We're having so much fun!"

I concurred. "We are having so much fun!"

The older couple got out of the upper hot tub, dried off, and grabbed their belongings off the chair. One of them said to me, "I just wanted to say that it was such a delight to hear how you talk to your daughter. You are so sweet with her. She's very lucky, and I wish you could train my daughter-in-law."

I was flattered by the kind compliment about my parenting and said, "Oh thanks," but then I felt bad about the daughter-in-law situation. Parenting is tough, and I like to think that everyone is doing their best. The comment hung out in the back of my mind while I got Zoomer out of the hot tub a few minutes later and dried off.

Before we left the pool area, I turned to the guest in the upper hot tub. "Want me to turn the dial again to keep the jets going?"

They said, "Yes, please," returned to their relaxed state, and closed their eyes.

"What are you doing, Mommy?" Z asked as I turned the dial.

"I'm turning on the jets again," I answered.

Zoomer looked toward the upper tub at the relaxed guest and said, "Our friend is sleeping!"

I smiled and nodded. "Yup, our friend is relaxing."

Thoughts were swirling in my head. Zoomer was regularly using they/them pronouns and the word *friend* or *person* to describe the new people we were seeing in Moab. I was happy that a stranger felt inclined to tell me they thought I was a good parent. I was proud of what a fun kid Zoomer has turned out to be and astonished by their narrative of the world. Of course, I'd been very consciously socializing Zoomer from the day they were born to have an inclusive perspective where gender didn't dominate, and I was finally seeing it pay off. As Zoomer had put it, I was "having so much fun."

Brent must have heard us galloping and hootin' and hollering down the hall because he greeted us at the door. Brent can always tell when something is on my mind; apparently, I have a very expressive face, and it gives away whatever emotions I'm feeling.

"What's going on in there?" Brent asked as he led Zoomer to the bathroom and took off their soaking wet diaper.

I told him about the couple at the pool and how they had complimented me on how sweet I was to Zoomer and that they wished I could train their daughter-in-law. I had so many follow-up questions.

I wanted to know if their adult child, the spouse of their daughter-in-law, was a good partner and an equally contributing parent. I wanted to know if their daughter-in-law felt trapped by parenthood or if she entered into it on purpose and at the right time. Was she fulfilled? Was she tired? Was she supported?

I feel so lucky to have a partner who equally shares parenting and all aspects of our household admin and income earning. We had planned for Zoomer, who is a very wanted child. We have resources, like stable careers that we love and full-time childcare, that make our lives easier. While our marriage isn't perfect, Brent and I are happy, and we love and respect each other and are committed to an egalitarian relationship. All those things make parenting easier and more enjoyable. Sure, there are some shitty parents in the world, but more often, there are shitty situations. I like to think that this daughter-in-law didn't need parenting "training." Maybe she just needed equally shared parenting and a break from the perfect-mom pressures of the world.

I sat on one of the beds, across from Brent and Zoomer, with a white pool towel wrapped around me. "It felt nice to have a stranger tell me I'm a good mom, someone who doesn't know who I am or what my parenting philosophies are. This person just saw me interacting with my kid and felt compelled to compliment me on what they saw."

Brent said, "You really are such an amazing mom, and Zoomer is so lucky to have you."

I smiled and looked down at my hands. "Thanks. It's just wild because, for the past year, strangers have said such terrible things about me online and told me that Zoomer should be taken away from me, all without knowing me or having any idea of what Zoomer's life actually looks like. Of course, there have been wonderful compliments from online strangers too, but a real-life stranger compliment felt validating and good. I make gourmet imaginary macaroni and cheese, for crying out loud! Mom of the year, I am!"

I stood up from the bed and asked Zoomer if they wanted to rinse all the spa chemicals off their body. They nodded, and as they strutted their naked little body toward the bathroom, they asked, "What's pa cheminals?" to which I tried to explain chlorine, which isn't as easy as it seems.

We climbed in the shower, and I handed Zoomer a bar of hotel soap. It had two rows of four semicircular bumps in it.

"This soap look like LEGO!" Zoomer announced.

I laughed because one of Brent's pet peeves is when people call LEGO *legos*. For some reason, making it plural with an *S* drives him bonkers. I made a mental note to tell Brent that he was raising his child right.

"It does, doesn't it?" Zoomer got straight to work, washing the shower tiles instead of their body. I called out to Brent and asked him to bring us a plastic cup so I could rinse the shampoo out of Zoomer's hair. Brent handed the cup to Zoomer. I tilted my head back into the running water and got my hair wet. When I looked down, Zoomer was holding the plastic cup, collecting the stream of water dropping off my pubic hair.

I laughed. "I wouldn't drink that if I were you."

Zoomer's hand lifted into the pointing gesture, and I could tell they were about to poke my vulva, which was right in front of their eyes. *Well . . . here's a teachable moment*, I thought.

"Zoomie, honey, it's not nice to poke someone's genitals without asking them first."

Zoomer paused, putting both hands around the cup, and looked up at me, squinting to keep the water out of their eyes.

I said, "Your body is your body, and my body is my body. I will only touch your genitals after you go potty or to help you clean yourself, OK?"

Zoomer nodded. "OK."

I grabbed the bar of soap off the floor of the tub and handed it to them. "Can you wash your body now?"

Zoomer nodded enthusiastically. "I wash off all the cheminals!"

Our life is full of little moments like this, where we can mention something in an age-appropriate way that sets the foundation for bodily autonomy, boundaries, and consent while normalizing anatomical terminology and celebrating how awesome our bodies are. Just the week before we went to Moab, Zoomer realized I had breasts. Mind you, they're perfectly inconspicuous breasts, but it's like Zoomer had forgotten about my breasts since the last time I nursed them when they were four months old. I was reading Zoomer a bedtime story, and they lay on my chest. Their head was met with a nice little pillow, in the form of my bra. They sat upright, looked at my chest, and pressed down on my bra and breast.

"What's this?" they asked.

"This is my chest area. I call these my breasts, and sometimes I wear a bra."

Zoomer made a "huh" sound, taking in this new information. "You have nipples?" they asked.

"I do have nipples," I confirmed.

They lay back down on my chest, said, "Me too," and lifted the *ABC's of Rock and Roll* book back up, asking, "What's the Go-Gos?" and "What's U2?" as we made our way through the alphabet.

We woke up in Moab on Monday morning to a fresh six-inch layer of snow. It was bittersweet getting in the car to head home. I had just had one of my favorite weekends of all time as Zoomer's parent, and I was sad that I'd be going back to work tomorrow morning, when all I really wanted to do was keep playing and exploring all day with Z and getting glimpses into the way they saw the world.

We had hiked the Park Avenue trail in Arches National Park the afternoon before. There were cairns, piles of stacked stones, intermittently along the trail.

"What's this tower?" Zoomer asked as we came across the first cairn.

"This is called a cairn. People stack rocks so that friends who come after them know where to go."

Zoomer grabbed a nearby stone, placed it gently on the stack, and said, "Zoomer should help?"

I smiled, and Brent said, "Yeah, sweetie, you can help."

All Zoomer's life, I had been building a foundation for them, little landmarks that they could look for to guide their way, something familiar that reassured them they were on the right track. Parents have an incredible responsibility to teach their children how to navigate in the world. My parenting cairns that I've spent the most time building include a beacon of acceptance, a beacon of love, a beacon of inclusivity, a beacon of open-mindedness, a beacon of fun, a beacon of respect, a beacon of compassion, a beacon of confidence, a beacon of self-awareness, and obviously, a huge beacon of macaroni and cheese.

During that magical weekend, Zoomer got involved in the stacking. Every time they used a gender-neutral pronoun for a stranger was the equivalent of them placing a stone on the inclusivity cairn. Each time they called a fellow hotel guest "friend" was a pebble on the compassion cairn. Not getting poked in the pubes felt like a big rock on the respect cairn.

Our family sat in the little theater at Moab Giants watching a documentary about dinosaurs, my hand on Zoomer's right leg and Brent's hand on Zoomer's left. Zoomer grabbed both our hands and held them, then looked at their parents through their oversize 3-D glasses with a smile on their face, and, gosh, the stones on the love cairn touched the moon.

TWENTY

Here We Are

Every night before climbing into bed, Zoomer picks out two books. Brent reads one, and I read the other. Zoomer is very picky about their books and is very specific about who reads what. I'll see the two books on their bed and say, "Aw! Great! I'll read you *Pizza Day*!"

And then Zoomer will say, very matter-of-factly, "No, Mommy. Daddy read *Pizza Day*. You read *All Are Welcome*." And then they'll hand me the book that they have picked out for me to read.

Zoomer also likes books in phases. They'll hand me the same book every single night for ten days. On night eleven, I'll go to grab the book I have pretty much memorized from reading it the last week and a half, and Zoomer says, "No, Mommy. Not that one. You read this one now, please," handing me a new book.

For Zoomer's second birthday, their friend Misha gave them the book *Here We Are: Notes for Living on Planet Earth* by Oliver Jeffers. At the time, Zoomer wasn't too into it, so it ended up on the bookshelf until almost a year later, twenty days before their third birthday. After their bath one evening, Zoomer made their way to the shelf, grabbed it, and handed it to me, and we climbed into bed to read it for the first time.

Here We Are is an adorably illustrated guide to Earth. There are pages with simple descriptions of the solar system and pages describing the land and sea. On one page, there is an illustration of a child, and the text says, "On our planet, there are people. One people is a person. You are a person. You have a body. Look after it, as most bits don't grow back." On the next two pages, there are illustrations of about eighty different people, and the text says, "People come in many shapes, sizes and colors. We may all look different, act different and sound different . . . but don't be fooled, we are all people."[30]

Every night for a week, I looked forward to getting to this page because I got a peek into how Zoomer was coming to understand the world and the people in it. They wanted to linger on the page for longer than any other.

"Mommy, let's count the people," they'd say, which I soon came to realize actually meant "Let's talk about the people" in Zoomer-speak. I'd point to the different people and describe something unique about them.

"This person is holding an orange balloon."

"This friend uses a wheelchair."

"This person is a beekeeper."

"This person is a mail carrier."

"This friend has a skateboard."

"This friend is in jail."

"This parent is carrying a baby."

"This one is an astronaut."

And on and on for eighty characters.

"That a ghost?" Zoomer asks.

"That person is wearing a burqa," I say, knowing Zoomer hadn't seen a burqa before.

"What's that called?" Zoomer asks, pointing to a child in western wear.

I search my brain quickly for a gender-neutral term for *cowgirl*. "That friend is a cowpoke, a buckaroo!"

Zoomer points to a person dressed in black, who is slouching over, looking a little down, and asks, "This friend sad?"

I nod. "They do look a little sad, don't they?"

Zoomer nods. "Yeah, maybe they sad." Zoomer is lying on their stomach. They rest their head on their hand and say, "Maybe that friend has a tummy ache and needs a hug."

I smile, so proud of the compassionate little person my child has become. "Shall we give them a hug?" I ask.

Zoomer leans down and hugs the book. "You better now, friend?" Zoomer asks the drawing.

"Do any of these people remind you of you, Zoomer?"

Zoomer scans the page of diverse people and lands on a child dressed in a red-and-purple superhero outfit and points.

"That's Zoomie, Zoomie a superhero."

"You *are* a superhero, Zoomie!"

I wanted to give my child a gift. The gift of understanding gender as complex and beautiful and self-determined and the gift of being free from the restrictions and limitations and expectations of binary gender and all the stereotypes that come with it. I hadn't considered how much of a gift I would also be giving myself.

Parenting is like being a tour guide. Parents help their children navigate the world, taking them to the great spots and steering them clear of unsafe ones. While curating an experience for Zoomer to explore their interests and come to their own identity, I inadvertently started taking a closer look at my own identity and how I operate in the world. Zoomer is a superhero; their superpower is ignoring the noise and seeing people for their individuality. Zoomer rescues people from stereotypes.

~

I imagine most parents don't remember the first time their child said "man" as vividly as I do. It was May 17, a couple of months after Zoomer's third birthday. Up until this point, I had never heard Zoomer use gendered words besides *Mom* and *Dad*. Everyone had just been a kid or a grown-up, a friend or a person. It was a Friday afternoon. I had picked Zoomer up from daycare, and we were in the car on our way home. I asked Zoomer how their day was, and they said, "Good. I saw a wheelbarrow."

I looked at them in the rearview mirror. "Oh, that's cool. Was it a toy wheelbarrow or a big wheelbarrow that grown-ups use?" I asked.

"It was the man's wheelbarrow."

My brain scratched like a broken record. *Oh gosh,* I thought to myself. *Zoomer just said "man." Why does this feel so weird?*

I asked, "A person was using a wheelbarrow?"

Zoomer said, "Yeah, a man."

They are making sure I know the person was a man.

"That's cool, honey. I'd love to know what *man* means to you," I said. Seeing if they would give me any insight into what that word meant to them. Not that I would be able to totally describe what the word even meant to me. I just wanted a peek inside their mind and how they were coming to understand gender.

"The man is James. James is a gardener," Zoomer responded.

"James is a gardener? That's neat. Was James planting pretty flowers at your school?" I asked.

"Yeah," Zoomer said.

I knew that one of their friends or teachers must have been using the word *man* to refer to James, and Zoomer was absorbing it, as kids do. I was grateful that I had had three years when I was able to teach Zoomer about people without getting into too many subcategories. Of course, gendered words were being used all around Zoomer, but they weren't picking up on them too much until after they turned three. I had been talking about gender in nuanced ways around Zoomer, and now Z was communicating about gender back to me.

"Did you get to talk to James? Was James nice?" I asked.

"Yeah," Zoomer responded, then looked out their window and said, "She was a nice man."

I was excited and nervous to be entering new gender creative parenting territory. I had spent the last three years narrating the world in a gender-expansive way, but now Zoomer was leading the conversation. I got to advance to a new level in teaching Zoomer about gender identity, gender expression, and pronouns and to help mold their understanding in real time. It's a common parenting experience, having to teach a child about a topic that is huge and nuanced, using simple but not reductive language to explain things like where babies come from or the death of a pet. It wasn't anything I couldn't handle; I just felt the pressure to get it right. I wanted Zoomer to think of gender like an infinite spectrum, not a binary category, and now I was going to be able to do that in a new way because they now understood that there was more to a person's identity. A person has a gender identity.

A friend of mine, Ari Dennis, introduced me to the term *ante-gender*, meaning *before* gender, like an anteroom is the space you are in before you enter a room.[31] In the first three years of Zoomer's life, they didn't need gender. They couldn't comprehend gender, at least not in the complex way I wanted to teach them about it. Gender creative parenting allowed for Zoomer to exist in an ante-gender space until they were ready to enter a new space, where they could ask questions and begin to think critically about gender.

In the ante-gender early years, I taught Zoomer about people as a generalized human species. Now we are stepping into a new phase, one where I will teach Zoomer that there are many different ways that humans can identify, and it's better to ask than to assume. I'm holding Zoomer's hand and leaving this ante-gender space, looking back on it fondly, like a first home, and excited for the next adventure.

~

Occasionally, Zoomer calls Brent and me by our first names, and it always makes me smile. The first time they did it was at Disney World when they were two. We were standing in line for the Jungle Cruise. Brent was holding Zoomer. It was the end of the night; we were all tired and having a quiet moment in the line between the ropes.

All of a sudden, Zoomer said, "Brent" and touched Brent's chest. Then they turned, pointed to me, and said, "Kyl." Brent and I looked at each other; our jaws dropped open in surprise. Zoomer was looking at a couple on the other side of the rope. Zoomer put their hand on their own chest and said, "Mimi," the cute way they were saying their name before they could pronounce *Z*s and *R*s, and then pointed to the two strangers they had just introduced their family to and waited patiently.

"I'm Esther. This is Diego. It's nice to meet you." And then the line moved, and our groups went in opposite directions. Zoomer laid their head down on Brent, and my eyes got a little watery. Zoomer is drawn to people, wanting to connect with them and know who they are.

Months after that first time I heard Zoomer say my name, we were playing a game of hide-and-seek at home.

Zoomer said, "Mommy, hide." They faced the wall, cupping their eyes so they couldn't see as I ran and hid in the pantry. They counted, "One, two, three, eight, seven, fourteen. Ready or not, I find you!"

Zoomer walked around the house, mimicking the words we use when we are trying to find them. "Mommy, you in the plant? No." "Mommy, you under the couch? No." As they got closer to the pantry, they called out, "Kyl! Where are you?"

Gender creative parenting comes with a complimentary giant mirror and forces me to confront and interrogate my own gender. Forces me to ask myself, "Kyl! Where are you?" I've examined my own gender identity and expression more in the last three years than I had in the three decades before becoming Zoomer's parent. As I've tried to create an environment where Zoomer is free from the chains of binary gender, I am working to untangle myself and trying to figure out what about my gender is authentic and what about my gender was prescribed to me, and is it even possible to differentiate at this point?

I'm trying to pull all the components of my identity off the shelves, take a good look at them, and determine if I like them and they should stay, or if they were thrust upon me and should go. I'm working through the traditional norms of being assigned female at birth. I love my body; however, I don't love that I was assigned a specific gender role because of it. I'm taking a good look at my habits related to grooming, makeup, and clothing—and the beauty standards that I have been inundated with since I was a child. I feel comfortable with the hair on my head being short, and the hair under my arms being long. It took a while, though, for me to find that comfort, after conforming to mainstream American beauty standards for as long as I can remember.

It's like a long list of feminine ideals sits before me, and I'm allowing myself to review it, to like some of the things on the list, dislike others, and to not feel bad about any of it. I love manicures; I can do without high heels; I like being athletic and alone; I don't feel like marriage and parenthood complete me or fulfill my destiny; there are so many other aspects to my purpose. I'm processing parts of my personality and behavior and trying to tease out my gendered performance in different settings, what parts of me feel genuine and what feels more like an act. I'm assertive and accomplished and unapologetic about it. I'm also tender and sensitive and want to laugh and learn. In my early thirties, I'm climbing out of the girl box I was placed in in 1986. I'm wandering around the gender spectrum, trying on new labels and pronouns, not necessarily looking for another box, just wanting to find my place as Kyl.

In giving Zoomer the gift of a gender creative childhood, we gave them a different perspective of the world than I had growing up, a perspective I hope they can hold on to throughout their life and share with others. I imagine what our world could be like—a world where gender diversity is celebrated, and gender-based oppression and violence don't exist. I think it's children like Zoomer who are going to be our superheroes. Instead of us telling the children who they should be, maybe it's the children who will teach us how to be. We just have to get out of their way.

~

When I was pregnant, I remember hoping that my and Brent's parents and siblings would be able to have meaningful connections with Zoomer. I was afraid that my family members might be so nervous about accidentally using a gendered pronoun for Zoomer, so nervous about offending me, that they would distance themselves from us. Thankfully, those fears of mine never manifested. Our family rallied around us, supported us in gender creative parenting, and they each formed their own special relationship with Zoomer.

My mom taught Zoomer how to make a pistachio cake that her grandmother used to make with her. When some bullies were going after us online, accusing me of being a bad parent, my mom jumped in and wrote love-filled retorts. I hear my mom use they/them pronouns for people she doesn't know. Our relationship is becoming stronger than it was before I became a parent.

My dad drove up to Salt Lake City the day I got out of the hospital after Zoomer was born and was the first family member to hold my new baby. My dad looks after Z when we go to Saint George, so Brent and I can go on a date. Zoomer and their grandpa soak in the hot tub and eat ice cream, and I return to find Zoomer cuddled up in the crook of my dad's arm on a recliner, watching a home renovation show on HGTV.

After spending a weekend visiting my grandmother in Oregon, my dad and I were driving to the Portland airport to catch our flights back to Utah. I thought of two-and-a-half-year-old Zoomer at home with Brent, then turned to ask my dad, "Has my decision to do gender creative parenting been difficult for you?" I watched as he thought for a moment, then he turned to me, shook his head, and simply said, "No." Then he returned his eyes to the coastal highway.

My bonus mom, April, gets down on the floor and plays with Zoomer for as long as Z wants, never acting like she has anywhere else to be. April has been an incredible advocate for us too, taking it upon herself to teach her family what gender creative parenting means. On the family ranch last Thanksgiving, we walked in, and I saw April's family members, whom I hadn't seen in years. They all said hello to me and Zoomer and were so warm and loving, asking us how we've been and commenting on how tall Z is getting.

April's twelve-year-old niece, Shelby, approached Zoomer and said, "Zoomer, do you want to go see the horses?" Then she looked up at me and said, "They can ride my horse if that's OK with you."

I was caught off guard by her natural ease using gender-neutral pronouns and how sweet she was to Zoomer, whom she had never met. I nodded. "Yeah, that's OK with me. Zoomer, do you want to ride Shelby's horse?"

Zoomer jumped up and down, excitedly said, "Yes!" and ran out the door with Shelby and the other tween-age cousins. I followed behind them, lifted Zoomer onto Echo's back, and held on to Zoomer while Shelby led Echo around the stable. I couldn't have imagined this situation while I was pregnant, scared of telling my parents, scared of the unknown. This was the unknown, though. Acceptance and affirmation.

Brent's parents adore their first grandchild. They send cards and presents from Australia and count down the days to seeing Zoomer every year. They visited us in Salt Lake and spent every single waking moment with Zoomer. When we visit them in Canberra, they play with Zoomer in the garden, teaching Z which tomatoes are ready to be picked and filling up the plastic pool that Zoomer happily splashes in naked. Zoomer helps their Mamma prepare dinner for the family, and then they snuggle on the couch, the couch where I felt Zoomer kick inside my pregnant belly for the first time, and they look through a photo album filled with pictures of Zoomer.

Zoomer and their Pappa have a running game of "I got you" where they try to scare one another. Z sneaks up behind Pappa, jumps out from behind the chair, and roars, and Pappa acts surprised while Zoomer laughs hysterically and says, "I got choo!"

Zoomer has a special relationship with each of their eight aunts and uncles. Brent's and my siblings hang out with Zoomer so we can go on dates, and they pay attention to what Zoomer is interested in to guide their conversations: conversations about riding bikes, about bath bombs, about hot chocolate, about going down the slide again, about wanting to blow bubbles and draw with sidewalk chalk. Our siblings, who range from very liberal to quite conservative in their beliefs, are all supportive of our gender creative parenting approach and love Zoomer.

I had been so nervous that gender creative parenting was going to strain my wonderful relationships with my family. But in hindsight, gender creative parenting has helped strengthen our relationships. I don't have to have awkward conversations with my parents about why I think they need to pump the brakes on stereotyping Zoomer because they are already consciously thinking about how they can incorporate gender creativity into the toys and clothes they buy Zoomer and the way they treat Zoomer.

The way our family uses gender-neutral pronouns and all sorts of adjectives for Zoomer and gets so involved in caring for them and loving on them makes my heart sing. I have gender creative parenting friends who haven't been as lucky. Some of my friends have lost touch with all their family members or have deeply strained relationships because of their decision to do gender creative parenting and their family's unwillingness to support them. I know of a grandparent who keeps a stash of clothing, so whenever their gender creative grandchild comes over, they change them out of the clothing the child picked out to put them in something more stereotypically associated with their sex.

Some of my friends' family members have called Child Protective Services, reporting their grandchild is being abused, simply because they weren't assigned a gender. A friend of mine was at a store with their gender creative child and ran into their sister, who they hadn't seen in months. She proceeded to use gendered pronouns and over-the-top gendered adjectives and words, publicly resisting and disrespecting my friend's decision to do gender creative parenting. Not everyone has had it as easy as Brent and I have. Which is also a reason I feel so strongly about being a public advocate for parenting this way—many others who are doing gender creative parenting don't have the safety, support, and resources to talk openly about it.

We sprang gender creative parenting on our families, and I hope someday I can find a way to thank them for their immediate acceptance. Our family made the decision to support us in our parenting plans, to understand gender creative parenting, and to get on board. Our family shared in shouldering the emotional labor of gender creative parenting and took it upon themselves to educate our extended family and their coworkers, neighbors, and friends so that we didn't have to do all the lifting. Our family members are champions at using gender-neutral pronouns. But even more importantly, our family has never treated Zoomer like a stereotype, never limited Zoomer's opportunities or shamed them for showing interest in something. Zoomer is showered in love and affection by their grandparents, aunts, uncles, and cousins. In my opinion, Zoomer Courtney-Myers hit the family jackpot.

TWENTY-ONE

Beautiful Princess Shark Man

The early years of gender creative parenting occur within a bubble. Virtually every single moment of my child's life was spent with Brent and me or in the care of another adult family member or teacher I trusted completely, who understood what gender creative parenting meant to us, and who consciously interacted with Zoomer without relying on stereotypes or a gendered script. Now, with every day Zoomer gets older, the protective, sheltering layer of the bubble gets thinner. I must trust that I've done enough to nurture Zoomer's confidence in themself, that I've instilled in them an inclusive perspective, and then surrender to how quickly kids grow up and allow the bubble to pop.

Eleven days after Zoomer's third birthday, just before midnight, we boarded a Fiji Airways plane in Los Angeles. We were headed to Viti Levu for a family vacation. I knew this trip would be a milestone for us. Zoomer was no longer our little baby. Zoomer was a self-identified big kid now. After a long flight and car ride, we arrived at the resort where we would spend the next six days.

"Bula!"

"Bula, princess."

"Bula, handsome!"

"Bula!"

Every time we passed a staff member, they greeted us with a "bula." The Fijian staff were incredibly warm and outgoing, especially with kids. Everywhere we went, the staff would take the time to acknowledge Zoomer, to ruffle their hair, to sneak them a treat, to tickle them, to bend down and ask Zoomer questions. They would assume a gender for Zoomer and then interact with them according to binary gender norms.

It was fascinating to watch one person treat Zoomer as a girl and the next treat them as a boy. "What's your name, beautiful princess?" the host at the restaurant asked.

"I'm Zoomer! I'm three!" Zoomer would respond.

We'd be seated for breakfast and then walk over to the smoothie bar, where the person behind the counter handed Zoomer a shot glass of paw paw smoothie and said, "This will make you swim faster, shark man."

Zoomer grabbed the smoothie and said, "Thank you." We walked back to our table, and I scooped up a spoonful of scrambled eggs to encourage Zoomer to eat. Zoom asked for more smoothie.

I shook my head. "If you eat a few bites of your eggs, you can have another smoothie." I looked at Brent and said, "Beautiful Princess Shark Man would drink a hundred shots of smoothie if we let them."

Over the course of the trip, Brent and I sat back a bit while Zoomer interacted with staff and other guests and kids. Zoomer was three. They were social. We wanted them to exercise some independence. Zoomer walked over to one kid, who let Z play with a Barbie doll in the pool for a few minutes. Zoomer walked over to another kid, who let Z play with a Marshall toy, the firefighter dog from *PAW Patrol*, for a while. Zoomer shared their multicolored diving sticks with other children, throwing them to a deeper end where either another kid or Brent or I would retrieve them. I could see adults look at Zoomer with tilting heads, unsure of how to gender them. Zoomer's long, golden hair cascaded down their back from underneath a light-pink sun hat. They had blue-and-pink sunglasses on, an aqua-colored long-sleeve rash guard, some board shorts with toucans on them, a blue Puddle Jumper life vest with a shark on the front, and purple sandals. Every single article, Zoomer had picked out. Some adults would say, "She's really cute." Others would say, "He's well behaved." Brent and I would smile and say, "Thanks."

One child, probably around six years old, was looking at Zoomer for a few seconds and then decided to approach Zoomer and me and ask, "Is this a boy or a girl?" I looked at Zoomer, who responded by making a clicking sound with their tongue a few times *clack cluck clack* and then paddled around me. I looked at the curious child, smiled, and shrugged my shoulders in a "Sorry, I can't help you out" kind of way, and I swam to catch up with Zoomer.

A few days into the trip, we went on a boat to Tivua Island.

"We offer snorkeling on the island," one crew member told us as they handed us a sign-up sheet.

I looked at Brent. "Snorkeling would be fun; do you want to go? We could trade off looking after Zoomer."

Just then, another staff member introduced herself. "Hi. I'm Salote. I'm here to look after the kids so you can do any activities you want on the island. What is your little one's name?"

"This is Zoomer," I responded.

"How old is she?" Salote asked.

"Just turned three," I replied.

Zoomer was wearing a black-and-white striped shirt, khaki shorts, a khaki hat, and purple sandals. I heard most of the crew members and staff using she/her pronouns when they were referring to Zoomer, the youngest child on the day trip.

"Thanks, Salote. I think we'll probably take you up on your offer so we can go snorkeling for a little bit."

Another guest on the boat took an interest in Zoomer. She asked Zoomer, "Can I take a picture with you, sweet princess?"

Zoomer was busy playing with their binoculars and didn't want much to do with her or anyone else for that matter; they had just discovered the little cakes laid out by the crew. The woman persisted. "You're so beautiful! You are such a beautiful girl. Do you want some candy?" That got Zoomer's attention, and they turned to look at the woman. Zoomer turned to look at me, making sure it was OK.

"You can have one piece of candy, Zoomer."

Zoomer walked up to the woman, who gave them a mint. Zoomer looked at the mint like they had been tricked. I could see they were thinking, *This isn't candy.*

"You are such a gorgeous princess. Do you want a flower in your hair? It will make you even prettier," she asked Zoomer.

I discreetly rolled my eyes a bit. Zoomer shook their head and said, "No, thanks."

As we neared the island, I scooped Zoomer up, and we headed to the front of the boat to get a look at Tivua. It was a small island that you could walk around the perimeter of in about six minutes, densely covered in palm trees, surrounded by white-sand beaches, a shallow reef, and turquoise-colored water. A long dock extended into the ocean, where the ship would anchor, and there was a small building where they prepared lunch, with volleyball nets nearby and hammocks strung from trees.

We got off the boat and headed to our little cottage that we had rented for the day. We changed into our swimsuits, lathered our pale skin in sunscreen, and headed toward the beach for some adventures. I found Salote and asked if she would be OK with looking after Zoomer for a half hour while Brent and I snorkeled.

"Of course! I'm happy to. We can go to the sandbox," she said. I watched her look down at Zoomer, and her head tilted to the side ever so slightly. I could tell she was taking in Zoomer's outfit—a white hat, the teal rash guard, the blue toucan shorts—and was second-guessing her previous assumption that Zoomer was a girl.

"Zoomer loves sandboxes. They'll like that," I said as I held Zoomer's hand and led them to the sandbox. Zoomer got settled into the sandbox, grabbed an orange plastic shovel in one hand, and started filling up an empty plastic water bottle with sand in the other.

I told Zoomer, "Mommy and Daddy are going to go in the water for a little bit. Salote is going to look after you, OK? We'll be back soon!" Brent and I walked toward the beach and along the dock with goggles, snorkel, and fins in hand.

After a while of snorkeling (and sorta hyperventilating because I'm terrified of the ocean), we heard a bell ringing, signaling that lunch was ready.

"I'm going to go get Zoom now," I told Brent.

"OK, I'll be there in just a minute! I'm going to take some photos," Brent said.

I returned my snorkeling gear to the hut and walked over to the sandbox. Zoomer was sitting at a tiny table and chairs with Salote, a paper plate full of food in front of them.

"Zoomer picked out all this food," Salote said, smiling, sitting on a little child's chair.

"That's cute. They love eating. Zoomer, do you want to come over to the big tables and eat with Mommy and Daddy now?" Zoomer nodded, smiling, with some potato salad smeared across their face. I grabbed Zoomer's plate and said, "Come on, honey." As Zoomer got up from the chair, they spotted Brent in the pavilion and ran toward him.

"Is Zoomer a girl or a boy?" Salote asked me as we walked toward the lunch buffet.

"Well, we do this thing called gender creative parenting. We didn't assign a gender to Zoomer when they were born; we just let them be a kid and give them the freedom to decide their own gender identity."

Salote was politely smiling at me, processing what I just told her, and not really knowing what to say next.

"Is there anything like that in Fiji?" I asked.

221

Salote shook her head. "No. Nothing like that." She didn't press me any further on it.

"Thanks for looking after Zoomer so we could snorkel. I really appreciate it, Salote."

"You're welcome," she said. "Enjoy the rest of your day on the island."

We played for a couple more hours, watching small reef sharks, trying to climb trees, and picking up some plastic out of the warm ocean, and then everyone boarded the ship to return to Nadi.

We had changed Zoomer into a lavender tank-top Wondersuit with pandas on it. Z was barefoot, and their hair smelled like sunscreen and sea salt. They pretended to steer the ship, holding on to the wooden wheel that was as tall as they were. They ate fresh coconut the crew cut for them. As Zoomer sat on the floor of the ship, drinking from a water bottle, the guest who had given them candy and offered a flower for their hair approached them.

"I'm confused," she stated. "Are you a girl, or are you a boy?" she asked Zoomer directly.

Zoomer looked up from their water bottle and said, "I'm Zoomie."

"But are you a girl or are you a boy?" she pressed.

"I'm three," Zoomer responded.

"But I want to know! Are you a girl or a boy?" she whined to our three-year-old.

Zoomer looked at her, and I heard them say, "A boy?"

I interpreted Zoomer's words as a question; they weren't very familiar with the term, and they wanted to know what it meant. The woman interpreted Zoomer's words as a statement of confirmation. I watched as a wave of relief washed over the woman, and then as that relief was sprinkled with minor betrayal.

"You're a boy? Why didn't you say something earlier when I was calling you princess? I was using the wrong words! You're a handsome prince!"

Zoomer had tuned her out and was busy fiddling with the lid of their water bottle. Now that Zoomer was a boy in her mind, she didn't want as much to do with them. I walked the few steps over to Zoomer and bent down. "Hi, honey. Are you all done?"

Zoomer nodded. "Yeah, I all done."

Whether we were talking about being done with the water bottle or the woman and all her questions, I don't know. Zoomer handed me the bottle, I lifted them up, and they wrapped their arms and legs around me. We sat down on a wooden bench and watched the ocean for a while.

"That was a little weird. Should we have stepped in earlier and said something to that woman?" I asked Brent later that night after we had gotten back to the resort, and Z was fast asleep.

Brent stopped grabbing all the clothes off the bed. "It was weird, but I think it's OK that we didn't intervene. I imagine Zoomer is asked if they are a boy or a girl by older kids at school. We just watched it happen for the first time."

I looked over at Zoomer, asleep on the sofa bed, their thumb in their mouth and their stuffed dog, Dante, in the crook of their arm. *How can they be so small and so big at the same time?* My baby wasn't really my baby anymore. I didn't need to speak on their behalf all the time, but they weren't past the point of needing me. We were in a state of transition. A new phase of *zwischen*. For the past three years, I had been creating an environment where Zoomer got to explore their interests without shame or coercion. I couldn't guarantee that the world was going to offer Zoomer the same unconditional love and freedom that our home had, and I had to surrender to that.

The next afternoon, Zoomer and I went to the resort pool. We were playing in the shallow end when a person's voice came over the loudspeaker: "Water aerobics will begin in two minutes."

"Oooh! Zoomie! Do you want to do water aerobics with me? It's like part exercise, part dancing, but in the pool," I asked excitedly.

Zoomer nodded and said, "OK, Mommy."

We swam to the area of the pool where some fellow guests and the aerobics instructor were standing. Zoomer's Puddle Jumper swim vest kept them afloat. Their little legs were treading water beneath them like a duck, and their arms and pruned fingers skimmed the surface of the water. *Oonz oonz oonz oonz*—the bass of the music started.

The Fijian instructor led us through a bunch of movements—five adults and a little smiling preschooler. We were reaching our arms to the sky, punching air, and kicking our legs underwater to the beat of a 1990s dance-pop song. Zoomer and I were following along, making silly faces at each other and laughing.

For a moment, time slowed down, and I tried to take it all in. I couldn't believe how far we'd come. Three years ago, I was in a pool with Zoomer in my belly, terrified of what our life was going to be like. Now I was in a pool with Zoomer beside me, this incredible child, so full of life, so self-aware, radiating positivity.

I wished I could have time-traveled back to 2016 and gotten in the pool with my pregnant self, desperately trying to flip her breech baby, floating in the water, silently worrying about what lay ahead. I'd tell her, "Yes, some of the things you're worried about happen, but you come out on the other side stronger and surer of the path you chose." I'd stroke her hair and say, "Spend more time thinking about the good stuff. Because this kid is the most amazing human you're ever going to meet, and being their parent is better than you can possibly imagine." I'd thank her for making a scary decision, for doing gender creative parenting despite all her fears, because it turned out to be the best parenting decision she's ever made.

EPILOGUE

I don't know what the future holds for us. In some ways, the first three years of gender creative parenting might have been the most difficult. I had to build my confidence up; I had to attempt to answer so many questions; I had to have faith that this was the right decision and stand my ground when swarms of strangers were convinced it was not. Every day that Zoomer got older, our life got a little bit easier. But I don't expect it to always stay that way. Maybe the next three years are going to really be the most difficult as Zoomer spends more time in the world without me, and my influence on Zoomer will be in competition with the influences of their peers, teachers, strangers, culture, and the media.

Zoomer is three and a half years old and has not identified with a gender yet, at least not out loud to us. I imagine we will be crossing that bridge within the next year or so as Zoomer's ability to communicate and ask questions develops parallel to their friends' declaring gender identities, expressions, and pronouns. I mention to Zoomer that, as they get older, they might identify as a girl, as a boy, or as nonbinary, or another gender term might fit them best. I let Zoomer know that their gender is up to them to decide and define. We're doing our best to help Zoomer understand that there is more to gender and sexuality than a binary. We're trying to help them think critically and creatively about gender and support them in their own evolution.

I am teaching Zoomer how to respect people's bodies, feelings, and personal space and to expect the same for themself. I am teaching Zoomer how to connect with friends on a deeper level and get to know what their friends are interested in, looking for traits and interests that make them special. I am teaching Zoomer how to navigate conflict, that hitting and pushing are not OK, and that friends don't hurt each other. I am teaching Zoomer how to share but also to claim their autonomy and right to what is theirs. I am teaching Zoomer that they and everyone around them deserve safety and not to experience violence and to let me or another grown-up know if they don't feel safe. Zoomer knows that they deserve affection and unlimited cuddles, but they also know that they don't have to give hugs or kisses if they don't want to, and neither does anybody else. I am teaching Zoomer to sing out loud, to wear whatever they want, and to live a vibrant, fabulous life.

These lessons have been consistent but rudimentary. Now that Zoomer is getting older, these teachings will also become more advanced. I want Zoomer to understand that these principles that I have been trying to instill in their life are tools for dismantling the patriarchy, White supremacy, classism, and ableism; for celebrating diversity and being inclusive and welcoming; for normalizing consent and autonomy; and for challenging systemic inequities and oppression. I want Zoomer to feel safe and deserving of practicing radical self-expression and love. I want them to have the confidence and support they need to discover and authentically live in their own identity and support others in doing the same.

Among my gender creative parenting friends who have older children, it seems that around the age of four, many of the kids start identifying with a gender and particular pronouns. My friend Zoë's oldest child, Aster, said that "he/him pronouns fit best" around his fourth birthday. At six, he says those are the pronouns that still fit best. He likes dressing in elaborate Tinkerbell and Harry Potter costumes. He helps kids around him understand that there's more than one way to be a boy; he calls himself a "bender boy." I still don't know anything about Aster's reproductive anatomy, because it's none of my business and not necessary to respect his identity and expression.

Aster's younger siblings, Oriole and Iva, are also being raised gender creative. Four-year-old Oriole prefers things that are pink and frilly and sparkly and told their parents that they are "a they/them." Oriole has noticed that when they are wearing dresses, no one comments on how smart they are, just how pretty. These children recognize the stereotypes in their world and push back on them, refusing to be put in any type of box while feeling confident in who they are.

Children raised with they/them pronouns and the freedom to explore gender grow up to have all types of identities and expressions. They all find pronouns that fit best—some use *she/her*; some use *he/him*; some use *they/them*; others want a combination, like *he/him/they/them*. Some choose new names for themselves. Most of the kids just want to be seen as individuals. As an Aster, an Oriole, a Hazel, a Scout, a Sojourner Wildfire, an Io, a Zoomer Coyote. The consensus among my friends with five-, six-, and seven-year-olds is that these children are growing up to have a more complex and inclusive understanding of gender. These kids feel confident in their identities and stand up for others.

Aster asked for a yellow Belle dress like the one from *Beauty and the Beast* for his fifth birthday, and his grandparents bought it for him. While out at a parade, some older boys pointed to Aster and said, "You can't wear dresses if you're a boy."

Aster smiled, holding the skirting in his hands, and said, "I can wear whatever I want!" The older boys paused. Of course boys can wear dresses. All kids should wear whatever they feel comfortable in. Our job as parents is to help kids celebrate diversity, not squash it.

The other day, Zoomer asked me if I was married. "Yeah, honey, I'm married to your dad, Brent."

Zoom sat on the bench in our entryway, putting their shoes on. They stopped and asked, "Did you wear a princess dress when you got married?" There must have been a pretend wedding on the play-ground or a teacher talking about going to a wedding that was sparking Zoomer's curiosity.

"No, I didn't wear a princess dress. Princess dresses aren't really my style. I wore a dark-blue jumpsuit. Want to see a picture?" I pulled out my phone and scrolled through photos until I found one on our wed-ding day and handed the phone to Zoomer. They held my phone and looked at the photo of their parents.

I said, "People get to wear whatever they want to get married in. And they can also marry whoever they want." Zoomer wasn't inter-ested in hearing a speech about marriage equality. They hopped off the bench and said, "Come on, Mom, there's a waterslide at school today." I smiled, knowing this is how it was probably going to be for a little while. Micro-opportunities to disrupt the gender norms they are hear-ing about at school or on TV.

I know Zoomer isn't going to exist in this beautiful bubble forever. The bubble where they can wear whatever they want and play with whatever they want and behave however they want without someone saying, "Wait, no, you don't get to do that." I'm trying to prepare myself for how difficult it will be to teach Zoomer that some people are scared of difference. That some people are mean to others who don't fit a ste-reotype. That some people hurt others.

I want to preserve Zoomer's carefree confidence. I dread the day that I hear Zoomer say something like, "I can't wear that anymore," or they let go of a toy they love and say something like, "I'm not supposed to play with this." I will help them understand that the gender binary is wrong, not Zoomer.

I imagine the next three years are going to be like the most intense game of Whac-A-Mole—where I try to smash the stereotypes, micro-aggressions, and inequities that pop up all day, every day. But in this round, Zoomer won't be protected behind me; I want them to be involved.

With Zoomer approaching their fourth birthday, Brent and I are researching the school district and possible elementary schools where Zoomer will start kindergarten. We want to find a place where Zoomer will be able to learn and thrive, that values inclusion and acceptance and supports the whole child. Regardless of how Zoomer identifies, I want them to be surrounded by adults and families who are trying to solve the world's problems, gender inequality included.

We're going to just keep taking this adventure one day at a time. Zoomer probably won't have many memories from the first three years of their life. I can't really remember much from my own early childhood. I hope when they are older, they pick up this book and read it from front to back. I hope they enjoy discovering this part of our family's story and can understand why we made the decisions and sacrifices that we did. I hope they read this as a love letter in a way. And this is just the beginning.

ACKNOWLEDGMENTS

It took a very special group of people not only to make this book happen but also to make everything that led up to this book happen.

To my parents, Renee Renick and Karlin and April Myers, thank you for raising me the way you did. I'm grateful for the autonomy you gave me to navigate through life and that you never shamed or doubted me when I ended up in areas and situations you hadn't expected I would. I am infinitely thankful for the freedom you gave me, and still give me, to find my way in the world. Thank you for coming on this gender creative parenting adventure with me and giving Zoomer a different kind of childhood. I hope I can convey to Zoomer how incredibly lucky they are to have you as grandparents. The love you have for Zoomer is palpable and radiates off you, making everything so positively warm. If I could bottle it up, I would—the world needs more of the type of love you give.

To John and Elizabeth Courtney-Frost. First, I must say thank you for raising Brent to be such a kind, compassionate, sensitive, honest, and talented man. You are both such wonderful people, and I am so fortunate to call you family and so grateful that you welcomed me into your life with so much love. You are the most incredible Pappa and Mamma to Zoomer, and I don't know if I will ever be able to convey how grateful I am that you trusted and supported Brent and me with our decision to do gender creative parenting.

Japheth, Mykenzie, Storie, D'Covany, Harlie, Tanner, Nathan, and Kimberley, thank you for being the best siblings to Brent and me and the most amazing aunts and uncles to Zoomer. I am grateful for your ease in supporting our little family and your commitment to contribute to the way we're raising Zoomer. Thank you for taking on so much emotional labor, for having countless conversations with the people who came to you with questions, for hanging out with Zoomer so Brent and I could go on dates, and for forming your own special relationships with your little nibling, Z. Thank you, thank you, thank you.

To all my Family Planning Division colleagues. Thank you for being one of the greatest parts of my life. I could not have written this book without your encouragement and patience. Thank you for being my friends, supporting work-life balance, and loving me and my family.

I have had incredible mentors and teachers. I am grateful for the faculty at Dixie State University, Riverside Community College, and the University of Utah, who saw something in me and challenged me to see it in myself and share it with others. My education was transformational, and I am especially grateful for the gender studies and sociology programs at the University of Utah, which really cracked my mind open and helped me put the pieces of my perspective together in a new and better way.

I am so grateful for the community that I found online through our Instagram account @raisingzoomer—I can't describe how special it has been to be supported by a network of strangers from across the globe, who became gentle teachers and loving friends.

To all my friends in the Parenting Theybies Facebook group, thank you for creating such a special community. I felt so alone when Zoomer was born, and I am forever grateful to Leah for introducing me to the community. I'm in awe of how much the movement has grown because of the emotional labor and love you all put into creating a more inclusive world for our children.

The majority of my story occurred on traditional native land. I want to acknowledge the indigenous peoples whose land was stolen from them. The Maricopa, where I was born; the Kalapuya, Paiute, and Navajo, where I was raised; the Ngunnawal and Gadigal people, where my partner, Brent, was born and raised and where we met; and the Shoshone, Goshute, Paiute, and Ute, where we live and raise our child.

Thank you, Alex Morris, for launching my story into the world through your writing.

Thank you, Christie Giera Allport, for introducing me to Jill Soloway, and Jill, for wanting to amplify my message. I'm so proud to be a part of the TOPPLE family and to contribute to toppling the patriarchy.

To my editor, Carmen Johnson, you are a legend, a hero, a magician. Thank you for shepherding this manuscript along through all its versions and for making it so much better. I have enjoyed getting to know you while you challenged me to dig deeper into myself. Thank you to Alex Kapitan, for your thoughtful feedback and suggestions; you truly are a radical copyeditor. Thanks, Philip Pascuzzo, for the perfect book cover.

Thank you, Chelsea, for being such an amazing friend to me since the day we met as doe-eyed undergrads. Your friendship sustains me.

Brent, where do I begin? Thank you for creating a life with me, for being open to this parenting idea I had, and for diving in and becoming the most committed, loving dad to our incredible kid. Thank you for showing me what true partnership could be. I am so grateful to be doing this whole life thing with you. Now, where's your mouth at?

Zoomer Coyote, this is for you. It's all for you.

ENDNOTES

Prologue

1   Kimberlé Crenshaw, "The Urgency of Intersectionality," TED Talk, posted December 7, 2016, www.youtube.com/watch?v=akOe5-UsQ2o.

2   Nikki Graf, Anna Brown, and Patten Eileen, "The Narrowing, but Persistent, Gender Gap in Pay," Fact Tank, Pew Research Center, March 22, 2019, www.pewresearch.org/fact-tank/2019/03/22/gender-pay-gap-facts.

3   "Gender Pay Gap Starts with Kids in America," BusyKid, June 29, 2018, https://busykid.com/2018/06/gender-pay-gap-starts-with-kids-in-america.

4   Kim Parker, Nikki Graf, and Ruth Igielnik, "Generation Z Looks a Lot Like Millennials on Key Social and Political Issues," Social Trends, Pew Research Center, January 17, 2019, www.pewsocialtrends.org/2019/01/17/generation-z-looks-a-lot-like-millennials-on-key-social-and-political-issues.

5   Margit Tavits and Efrén O. Pérez, "Language Influences Mass Opinion toward Gender and LGBT Equality," *Proceedings of the National Academy*

of Sciences 116, no. 34 (August 2019): 16781–86, www.pnas.org/content/116/34/16781.

6   Elizabeth A. McConnell, Michelle A. Birkett, and Brian Mustanski, "Families Matter: Social Support and Mental Health Trajectories among Lesbian, Gay, Bisexual, and Transgender Youth," *Journal of Adolescent Health* 59, no. 6 (December 2016): 675–80, www.ncbi.nlm.nih.gov/pubmed/27707515.

Chapter Two

7   H. Dean Garrett, "The Three Most Abominable Sins," in *The Book of Mormon: Alma, the Testimony of the Word*, ed. Monte S. Nyman and Charles D. Tate Jr., 157–71 (Provo, UT: Religious Studies Center, Brigham Young University, 1992), https://rsc.byu.edu/archived/book-mormon-alma-testimony-word/10-three-most-abominable-sins-0.

8   German Lopez, "Utah Just Repealed a Law That Banned Teachers from Talking about Gay People in Classrooms," Vox, March 21, 2017, www.vox.com/identities/2017/3/8/14855342/utah-no-promo-homo-law.

Chapter Three

9   Susan B. Sorenson, "Gender Disparities in Injury Mortality: Consistent, Persistent, and Larger Than You'd Think," *American Journal of Public Health* 101 (Suppl 1) (December 2011): S353–58, www.ncbi.nlm.nih.gov/pmc/articles/PMC3222499.

10   Holly Hedegaard, Sally C. Curtin, and Margaret Warner, "Suicide Rates in the United States Continue to Increase," US Department of Health and Human Services Centers for Disease Control and Prevention,

National Center for Health Statistics, NCHS Data Brief no. 309 (June 2018), www.cdc.gov/nchs/data/databriefs/db309.pdf.

11   Helene Schumacher, "Why More Men Than Women Die by Suicide," BBC, March 17, 2019, www.bbc.com/future/story/20190313-why-more-men-kill-themselves-than-women.

12   Claude M. Steele, *Whistling Vivaldi: How Stereotypes Affect Us and What We Can Do* (New York: Norton, 2011).

13   Lin Bian, Sarah-Jane Leslie, and Andrei Cimpian, "Gender Stereotypes about Intellectual Ability Emerge Early and Influence Children's Interests," *Science* 355, no. 6323 (January 27, 2017): 389–91, https://science.sciencemag.org/content/355/6323/389.

14   Deborah J. Vagins, "The Simple Truth about the Gender Pay Gap," *AAUW*, Fall 2018, www.aauw.org/resource/the-simple-truth-about-the-gender-pay-gap.

15   Carolyn de Lorenzo, "The Gender Pay Gap Might Start with Children's Allowances, a New Report Suggests," Bustle, July 10, 2018, www.bustle.com/p/the-gender-pay-gap-might-start-with-childrens-allowances-a-new-report-suggests-9715383.

16   Lisa Selin Davis, *Tomboy: The Surprising History and Future of Girls Who Dare to Be Different* (New York: Hachette, in press), www.lisaselindavis.com/tomboy.

Chapter Four

17   Shelley Correll, Stephan Benard, and In Paik, "Getting a Job: Is There a Motherhood Penalty?" *American Journal of Sociology*

112, no. 5 (March 2007): 1297–338, http://gap.hks.harvard.edu/getting-job-there-motherhood-penalty.

Chapter Six

18 Jana Studelskan, "The Last Days of Pregnancy: A Place of In-Between," *Mothering*, April 10, 2012, www.mothering.com/articles/the-last-days-of-pregnancy-a-place-of-in-between.

19 "Breastfeeding Info: Transgender and Non-Binary Parents," La Leche League International, www.llli.org/breastfeeding-info/transgender-non-binary-parents.

20 Lance Allred, "What Is Your Polygamy?" TEDxSaltLakeCity, TEDx Talks, posted October 7, 2016, www.youtube.com/watch?v=MbXzVrzTXHQ.

21 Piper Christian, "Tell a Story, Protect the Planet," TEDxSaltLakeCity, TEDx Talks, posted October 7, 2016, www.youtube.com/watch?v=wJq2lpeb3rQ.

22 Kyl Myers, "Want Gender Equality? Let's Get Creative," TEDxSaltLakeCity, TEDx Talks, posted October 7, 2016, www.youtube.com/watch?v=12t7PYilNQQ.

23 Alex Morris, "It's a Theyby!" *New York*, April 2018, www.thecut.com/2018/04/theybies-gender-creative-parenting.html.

24 Amy Packham, "Gender Creative Parenting: A Mum Explains Why She's Not Disclosing Her Child's Sex," HuffPost UK, April 10, 2018, www.huffingtonpost.co.uk/entry/gender-creative-parents-what-to-know_uk_5acb5696e4b0337ad1e9f726.

25   Budd Rishkin, "'Theybies': Letting Children Decide Their Gender," *On Point*, recorded July 24, 2018, www.wbur.org/onpoint/2018/07/24/theybies-children-gender-designation.

26   Holly Wainwright, Jessie Stephens, and Mia Freedman, "Get Your Chin Hair Out," produced by Elissa Ratliff, *MamaMia Out Loud*, podcast, April 10, 2018, www.mamamia.com.au/what-is-a-theybie.

27   Mia Freedman, "Kyl Myers Is Letting Her Child Decide Their Gender," produced by Elissa Ratliff, *No Filter with Mia Freedman*, podcast, August 26, 2018, https://omny.fm/shows/no-filter/kyl-myers-is-letting-her-child-choose-their-gender.

28   Kyl Myers, "Gender Creative Hair," www.raisingzoomer.com/article/gender-creative-hair.

29   Emily R. Mondschein, Karen E. Adolph, and Catherine S. Tamis-LeMonda, "Gender Bias in Mothers' Expectations about Infant Crawling," *Journal of Experimental Child Psychology* 77, no. 4 (December 2000): 304–16, www.ncbi.nlm.nih.gov/pubmed/11063631.

Chapter Twenty

30   Oliver Jeffers, *Here We Are: Notes for Living on Planet Earth* (New York: Philomel Books, 2017).

31   Nama Winston, "'You Got It Wrong': Sparrow and Hazel Are Being Raised by Multi-Adult Parents as 'Theybies,'" *MamaMia Out Loud*, podcast, May 19, 2019, www.mamamia.com.au/what-is-a-theyby.

ABOUT THE AUTHOR

Photo © 2019 Brent Courtney

Dr. Kyl Myers is a sociologist, educator, and globally recognized advocate of gender creative parenting. Kyl's TEDx talk, "Want Gender Equality? Let's Get Creative," encourages people to rethink childhood gender socialization in an effort to break up the binary before it begins. Kyl is the creator of www.raisingzoomer.com and the Instagram account @raisingzoomer. Kyl lives in Salt Lake City, Utah, with their family. For more information, visit www.kylmyers.com.